T5-AGU-549

Family in America

Family in America

Advisory Editors: David J. Rothman

Professor of History,
Columbia University

Sheila M. Rothman

MARRIAGE

IN THE

UNITED STATES

BY AUGUSTE CARLIER

$\mathcal{A}$RNO $\mathcal{P}$RESS & $\mathcal{T}$HE $\mathcal{N}$EW $\mathcal{Y}$ORK $\mathcal{T}$IMES

New York   1972

Reprint Edition 1972 by Arno Press Inc.

LC# 70-169376
ISBN 0-405-03853-4

Family in America
ISBN for complete set: 0-405-03840-2
See last pages of this volume for titles.

MARRIAGE

IN THE

UNITED STATES,

BY AUGUSTE CARLIER,

AUTHOR OF "L'ESCLAVAGE DANS CES RAPPORTS AVEC L'UNION AMERI-
CAINE," AND "HISTOIRE DU PEUPLE AMERICAIN. ETATS-UNIS
ET DE SES RAPPORTS AVEC LES INDIENS DEPUIS LA
FONDATION SES COLONIES ANGLAISES
JUSQU'A LA REVOLUTION DE 1776."

TRANSLATED FROM THE FRENCH BY

B. JOY JEFFRIES, A.M., M.D.,

Fellow of the Massachusetts Medical Society ; Member of the American Medical Association ;
Surgeon to the Massachusetts Charitable Eye and Ear Infirmary ;
Physician to the Boston Dispensary.

BOSTON:

DE VRIES, IBARRA & CO.,

PUBLISHERS, 145 TREMONT STREET.

———

NEW YORK: LEYPOLDT AND HOLT,

451 BROOME STREET,

1867.

TABLE OF CONTENTS.

PAGE.

INTRODUCTION xi

CHAPTER I.

MARRIAGE IN FRANCE.

I. — How it takes place 1
II. — Civil Capacity and Legal Ceremony 3
III. — Religious Marriage Ceremony 4
IV. — Indissolubility of Marriage. — Separation from "bed
and board" 4
V. — Condition of the Wife 7
VI. — Position in Society 9
VII. — Participation in Business 10
VIII. — Marriage considered as an Element of Population . 11

CHAPTER II.

MARRIAGE IN ENGLAND.

I. — Preliminaries 13
II. — Celebration of Marriage in England 16
III. — Gretna Green 18
IV. — Marriage in Scotland 19
V. — Position of the English Wife 20
VI. — The Domestic Hearth turned into a Boarding-house. 21
VII. — Society Life 23
VIII. — Civil Rights of the English Woman 24
IX. — The English Woman considered as an Heir 25
X. — Divorce, and Separation from Bed and Board, in
England 26

CHAPTER III.

MARRIAGE IN AMERICA.

	PAGE.
I. — Preliminaries	31
II. — Civil Capacity for Marriage Celebration	35
III. — Eccentric forms of Celebration	38
IV. — Mock Marriages	39
V. — Forced Marriages	40
VI. — Marriages in the West	44
VII. — Misalliances	46
VIII. — Forced Marriages. — Elopements	48
IX. — Aristocratic Tendencies	51
X. — The Law Favoring Fraud	53
XI. — Situation of the American Wife. — Revolt against the Laws of Marriage	56
XII. — Protestation against the Law by the Pastor who performs the Ceremony	62
XIII. — Considerations of Inheritance. — The Rights of Women	64
XIV. — The Family and its Deviations in the North	66
XV. — Domestic Life in the South	70
XVI. — Emigration into the Interior. — Dispersion of Families	71
XVII. — Education of the American Family	73
XVIII. — Reforms in the Condition of the American Woman	76
XIX. — The Female Physician	78
XX. — Women as Ministers of Religion	81
XXI. — The Desirable Role for the American Woman	84
XXII. — Prohibition of Marriage with Colored People	87
XXIII. — Marriage of Slaves between themselves Prohibited by Law	89
XXIV. — Counterfeit of Marriage with Mulattresses ?	92
XXV. — Mormons	97
XXVI. — Celibacy Proclaimed as a Principle by the Shakers	98
XXVII. — Divorce	100
XXVIII. — Numerous Causes for Divorce	104
XXIX. — Decision Left to Tribunals. — Divorces Decreed by the Legislature	106
XXX. — English and American Laws of Divorce Compared	108

PAGE.

XXXI.— Prohibition of Divorce. — Concubinage Legalized
in South Carolina . . . ./ 109
XXXII.— Divorces Numerous 111
XXXIII.— Legitimation by a Subsequent Marriage Prohibited. 117
XXXIV.— Have Democratic Institutions had a Marked Effect
on the Family. — What is Woman's Influence in
American Society. 120
XXXV.— Tendency of Morals Fatally Opposed to the Purpose
of Marriage 151
XXXVI.— Model Families 161

APPENDIX.

I.— On the Marriage of Ministers. — The Ceremony Per-
formed by Themselves 165
II.— Upon Manners at Watering Places 166
III.— Increase of the Number of Female Ministers of Re-
ligion 168
IV.— Statistics Concerning the Mormons 168
V.— Sect of the Shakers 170
VI.— With regard to the Number of Divorces 176
VII.— Upon the Increase of Population in the United
States 178

TRANSLATOR'S PREFACE.

MR. CARLIER, the author of this book, travelled some time in this country, observing our manners and customs, and studying our institutions. Familiar with our language, and recognizing our peculiarities and prejudices, he was enabled to see a great deal of our life not generally or readily got at by foreigners. He has made himself master of our political, religious, and social history, as is proved by the books he has since written, namely, "Slavery in its Relations to the American Union," and "History of the American People : the United States and their Relations with the Indians, from the Foundation of the English Colonies up to the Revolution of 1776." He is now engaged in the preparation of a work on the *institutions* of the United States.

To us, New Englanders especially, that man must seem rather bold who dares attack De Tocqueville's statements and deductions in his "Democracy in America." Yet, if one will read carefully and weigh without prejudice what Mr. Carlier has written simply on the point of marriage alone, he must needs admit that De Tocqueville's views can only be reconciled with the truth, if it is granted that what he says of our country shall be considered as applying, in great part or alone, to New England. De Tocqueville said, " There is certainly no country in the world where the tie of marriage is so much respected as in

America, or where conjugal happiness is more highly or worthily appreciated. In Europe, almost all the disturbances of society arise from the irregularities of domestic life."

At present, this seems hardly true, even of New England. We must admit, therefore, the force of Mr. Carlier's reasoning, however unpleasant it may prove to our national pride. Objection may be made, that the author's statements are based upon newspaper authority. But the journals give official reports and statistics, and these, of course, correctly, whilst editorial remarks and criticism show how the popular wind is blowing. Newspapers, although they apparently form, yet really simply represent public opinion. If any one doubts Mr. Carlier's deductions in reference to divorce, etc., they need only do as I have done, — namely, cull from the various papers the official reports of the courts of law on these points, — and they will probably find, as I did, that the task was too unpleasant to be pursued.

Certainly the last six or seven years have not much remedied the defects and omissions in the laws on marriage and divorce. In some of the Western States, the laws of divorce render marriage temporary concubinage; and, in some of the Eastern States, greater privileges in regard to holding property are granted the married woman, to enable the husband to *set aside* in her name what really belongs to his creditors.

Except in one or two instances, I have refrained from comment upon Mr. Carlier's deductions, and not thought it necessary to correct inaccuracies arising from changes in our political condition caused by the rebellion. It is to be remembered that the author wrote his remarks on the relations of the white to the colored race seven years ago.

Although some time has elapsed since this book was published, there will be found a certain freshness in it, to be accounted for, I think, by the fact, that, as a mental reaction after our civil war, earnest spirits and active minds are again turning their thoughts towards the social questions beginning to be discussed previous to the rebellion. We can hardly take up a newspaper or journal, published during the last few months, without finding some paragraph touching upon these topics. Certainly, marriage and the social and legal relations of the sexes demand the best brains and the truest enthusiasm of reformers, tempered by the conservatism of New England, and enlightened by the truths of modern science. May not a hope be expressed, that these great questions will not be taken up and discussed for the purpose of small personal notoriety, or as a field for oratorical display, — much as, Mr. Carlier says, was the fate of that paramount question, the abolition of slavery ?

But why, some friend will ask, put before people in bad English what was written in good French? I reply, Those familiar with French would never, perhaps, take the trouble to read the original, and may, like those unfamiliar with the language, be somewhat attracted by the idiom and crudeness of a translation. No one, I believe, can read this book and ponder its contents, without a feeling of concern for our present and foreboding for our future social relations. Let us, at any rate, remember that " opposition should excite attention and not anger."

B. JOY JEFFRIES, M.D.,

MARCH 1, 1867.   15 Chestnut St., Boston.

I append an extract from a letter of the author.

PARIS, Dec. 12, 1866.

CHER MONSIEUR, — Je ne vois rien pour le moment
à ajouter à mon livre le *Mariage aux Etats-Unis*, donc
vous avez fait la traduition. La publication presque im-
médiate rendait effectivement mon concours impossible,
mais je vois avec plaisir que vous avez pu vous en passer,
et qu' ainsi je ne serai cause d'aucun retard.

Je desire apprendre que votre travail obtient tout le
succès qu'il mérite, surtout à raison de l'idée-mère qui a
determine votre publication. C'est ainsi que par les
efforts combinés des gens de cœur des deux côtés de
l'Atlantique, on peut espérer venir en aide à la morale
publique et aux réformes urgentes que réclame l'état de la
société, maladif partout, mais non incurable, du moins
il faut l'esperer.

Je vous autorise à publier ce qui précéde, si cela vous
parait utile. Recevez, cher monsieur, avec tous mes
remerciements, l'assurance de mes sentiments empressés.

A. CARLIER,
6, Rue de Milan.

INTRODUCTION.

OF modern nations, the North Americans are perhaps the people most fortunately circumstanced and favorably situated to influence the future of the world. In whatever point of view we regard America,·there is a vast and ever-increasing field of study for the philosopher, the historian, and the economist. We cannot look with indifference upon the progress of a nation whose population less than a century ago did not exceed three millions, and which will reach eighty millions at the close of this. An asylum precious to all unfortunates, a vast arena for every ambition, placed midway between Europe and Asia, this country is called to incalculable destinies, — all the more important, as under their guidance everything marches onward with lightning-like rapidity. The American people believe in a divine mission : the future will tell how they fulfil it.

Till now, politics, political economy, philosophy, and literature are the only aspects of American life which European, or I should rather say French, writers have more closely examined; for nothing among our neighbors approaches the works of MM. de Tocqueville, Michael Chevalier, and other talented authors, too numerous to mention. This sphere of human activity presents such extensive views, such momentous problems, that the mind takes delight in them, where it may roam without restraint. And yet these subjects of investigation are for the United

States almost wholly modern. They do not extend farther back than the Confederation, which gave such a strong nationality to the English colonies, till then isolated from each other and having nothing in common but the yoke which they shook off.

Two fundamental institutions, however, have not seemed to attract the same amount of attention, and yet their study is susceptible of an equal degree of development with the other subjects already investigated, and which, being the basis of all society, have as great, if not a superior, claim upon the meditation of the moralist, — I mean religion and the family. Treated at length, these subjects would lead to very extended investigation ; but, if the examination does not touch somewhat upon practical life, the reader might remain unacquainted with important facts, the hidden springs of a great ensemble. These facts are, moreover, of great value in showing the precise point on this path which the Americans have reached since the foundation of the colonies. Nothing exhibits more clearly the irregularities of public morals while connected with events which hurry on, rather than succeed, each other in this country, and against which it has opposed but a frail barrier.

There is an important circumstance here which gives peculiar interest to this investigation, — namely, the elements which formed the first nucleus of the colonies. It will be remembered, that their origin and growth resulted from the persecutions following the religious wars which harassed Europe in the seventeenth and eighteenth centuries. The victims of these persecutions, of whatever sect, even the Catholics, sought in this land, then unknown to civilization, a refuge for their ardent faith. The population therefore at the commencement, and even afterwards, was mostly composed of men of religious charac-

ter, strongly imbued with the ideas of right and duty, —
with them inseparable constituents of every healthy social
organization.

Religion was so peculiarly mingled with all the circumstances of civil life, that many matters of legislation spe-
cially referred to the Bible, which became, so to speak, the
corpus juris of the New England immigrants. Wherever
religious sentiment had been cultivated, the family circle
was strong, because it was united, and the father, who
resembled somewhat the patriarch of old, possessed an
authority, not only undisputed, but even revered; for it
was composed of benevolence and justice, two attributes
which the mind is always pleased to reverence. Marriage
formed the family. It was a sacred union in which the
whole community was interested, and from this relation
became an institution of the highest character. It was
contracted under the eyes and with the approbation of the
head of the family, and consecrated by the pastor in
accordance with the imperative prescriptions of the law,
but always in obedience to a recognition of religious duty.
Nothing but their own happiness influenced the choice of
the espoused, and the union was perpetual, to be severed
only by death.

In England, the country which furnished the first and
larger proportion of colonists, marriage had always been
greatly respected. It was considered an abundant source
of wealth and population, the centre of all the affections,
and a most excellent school for morals and the appren-
ticeship of life. Hence, we need not wonder at seeing
in the primitive laws of the New England colonies, where
the religious sentiment was so intimately associated with
the idea of family, the most severe penalties pronounced
against violations of conjugal life. In the eyes of these
pious men, the family was the great pillar of society, — if

one became enfeebled, the weakness of the other followed ; but, if the family was firmly based, then the community would flourish and be prosperous.

It is true, that every epoch has its peculiar features,
and that the great development of centres of civilization
has necessities not compatible with much austerity. Yet
may we not admit less severity of life according to the
age, and at the same time hold fast those things which
are essential to the family, — namely, absolute guaranties
preceding and accompanying the conjugal tie, respect for
parental authority, and the domestic hearth always lighted
up and vivified by the intimate reunion of the members
who compose it ?

The true way to appreciate the change which religion,
marriage, and the family have undergone in the United
States is to compare their actual condition with the sketch
which I have given of their former state. In the investigation which follows, I shall be obliged to forbear the
question of religion, as it alone would require a special
and extended examination. I shall limit myself to inquir-
ing what marriage is at the present day ; whether society
has surrounded it with those guardian precautions which
are requisite to insure its durability, or whether the personal independence resulting from democratic institutions
has not acted unfavorably upon it. I shall speak of the
home or fireside as it now is, and explain how the family
organization has altered. I shall show that the consideration of race has exercised a deplorable influence, by
the prevention of certain unions, and by its pernicious
influence upon private morals. Divorce will be seen
to have an important place in this examination, and will
be found to be of no small importance in affecting the
condition of marriage. And I shall finally show, that
what the ancients considered the principal purpose of

marriage is seriously perverted, and how necessary it is to
re-establish to its proper position so important an institution, on which, unfortunately, the same degree of respect
is not now bestowed as formerly.

Since the Americans and English are of the same race,
I shall precede this investigation by some remarks upon
marriage as it exists in England. The first colonists carried the English form of marriage to America. It has,
however, been since modified on both sides of the Atlantic.
It remains, therefore, to ascertain which of these two peo-
ples has been more successful in its reforms.

I shall sketch, also, marriage as it is in France, in order
to better show, by a comparative examination, what this
institution is in the United States. This investigation,
wholly an analysis, is perhaps of itself somewhat unprofit-
able, and only redeemed by the interest which the reader
will find in becoming acquainted with facts, generally, I
believe, unknown in Europe.

CHAPTER I.

MARRIAGE IN FRANCE.

I.

How it takes place.

I COMMENCE with marriage in France.

With us, the paternal authority has remained tenderly patriarchal. The mother watches with constant vigilance over the development of her daughter's character and feelings. Never leaving her, she becomes her natural companion. All the treasures of her affection are constantly lavished upon her, as though it was her duty to remove every thorn that might spring up in the path of her child. Perhaps this kind of protection lasts too long, like the leaf which is destined to guard the gradual development of the fruit, whose too protracted shade but retards its ripening. It may be said that the mother recognizes this condition, and the responsibility resulting from it, as she rather hastens the marriage for which her daughter is scarcely yet prepared. It is true that, without pressing her feelings upon her, she is her guide ; yet it must be confessed that, being always spared anything that might trouble her life, the young girl cannot acquire that habit of perception and appreciation which constitutes true responsibility, so that her decision becomes less a matter of choice than of acceptance.

This early marriage, and absence of spontaneousness on the part of one who is engaging her future forever, are strongly criticised, both by the Americans and the English, who cannot see in it any assured guaranty of happiness. Be that as it may, in such a marriage the young girl very often consents, less from natural attraction than considerations of position, which cause the first defloration of her heart. It is here that the law intervenes.

Although well known to every one in France, I will here give the substance of it, in order to contrast its foresight with the indifference of the American law.

II.

Civil Capacity and Legal Ceremony.

The minimum age required by French law is eighteen years for the husband, and fifteen for the wife. There is also required the consent of the betrothed, that of the parents of both parties, or, if there are none, that of the grandfathers or grandmothers ; and even the assent of the counsel of the nearest relation, where there are no ascendants. In case of refusal, the ceremony cannot take place unless the man is twenty-five years old and the woman twenty-one, and the one to whom consent has been refused must seek assent by judicial procedure. The marriage must be preceded by a publication of the banns, registered at the offices of the competent *maires;* and is not valid unless performed by one of these *maires*, at his office, in the presence of four witnesses. The act must be signed by the parties, the witnesses, and the *maire.* It is, moreover, recorded in two special registers, one of which is deposited in the archives. Such is the substance of the law which sanctions and governs marriage in France.

III.

Religious Marriage Ceremony.

Independent of this legal marriage, which is accompanied with no external solemnity, Catholics and Protestants, guided by spiritual impulse, have called upon religion for its special benediction. Among Catholics, with whom marriage is a sacrament, no one will deny that the ceremonies of the church impress upon this important act of life such a character of solemnity as to often leave deep and lasting impressions.

IV.

Indissolubility of Marriage. — Separation from "bed and board."

The law, in accordance with Catholic doctrine, declares marriage to be indissoluble. The only way open to the married, when living together has become impossible, in cases determined by law, is the "separation from bed and board." But Americans and English consider that this separation punishes the innocent more than the guilty, and admits the danger of children with doubtful, if not criminal, paternity,— a paternity very often disputed, and one which an injured husband cannot always prevent or disclaim.

No doubt this separation is not free from some of the defects with which it has been charged, and which it would perhaps be easy to remedy. It has, however, advantages not to be overlooked ; the proof being the part which it plays in the bill of reform passed in England in 1857, as we shall hereafter see. Opinion, therefore, in America, is certainly wrong in rejecting this expedient, which in certain cases may very properly supply the place of divorce, so common in that country.

Nevertheless the number of separations *de corps*, as that of divorces, is a sort of test of the selection which presides over marriages, and of the greater or less harmony existing among married people. In this relation we regret to say, that, in France, the separations from "bed and board" multiply in a ratio by no means in accordance with the gradual increase of population. The Minister of Justice, in his last Report of the "Administration of Civil Justice" in France for the year 1858,* declares that the number of petitions for separation *de corps*,

* Moniteur, 17 Avril, 1860.

which was not more than one thousand to eleven hundred a year between 1851 and 1855, rose in 1857 to seventeen hundred and twenty-seven, and in 1858 to nineteen hundred and seventy-seven.

If we look for the cause of such applications, we shall find that, of these nineteen hundred and seventy-seven, eighteen hundred and twenty-seven originated from ill-treatment or serious injury, and only two hundred and twenty-three on account of adultery; which would seem to show that the majority of the petitions came from the lower classes, and, moreover, that conjugal fidelity is better observed than certain detractors allow.

An important point arising from this investigation is, that of this large number of petitions, seventeen hundred and seventy-seven are made by wives, and two hundred only at the suit of husbands.

Moreover, the Report states that the tribunals granted only fourteen hundred and ninety-two, and rejected two hundred and twelve, leaving two hundred and seventy-two which were either withdrawn or abandoned.

We would not from this infer, that the misfortunes of marriage are to be found within the limits of statistics. Not at all. It must be remembered that there are in addition, in France as elsewhere, outside of this class, those who separate by mutual consent to avoid the publicity of the court; and those who with deep regret assume the appearance of a supportable position, withdrawn from all observers, preferring the protection of the domestic hearth to an amicable separation, for the sake of the growing family in whose interest this great sacrifice is made. These occurrences, however, being common to all countries, we would confine ourselves to the official returns, which will serve to compare analogous conditions in the United States.

Let us see what is the position given the wife by law and by custom.

V.

Condition of the Wife.

The wife is in every respect the equal of her husband; he is in no way superior to her, except in their civil relation, in carrying on their common interests : the wife, however, is not ignored by this, for *her* consent is indispensable, and she has a right to be consulted, in certain cases, with the power of absolute veto. She retains the ownership of her whole fortune, there being some reservation as regards personal property.

The profits accruing from the industry of the husband and wife, and their savings, belong to them in common, the latter owning one-half. The law has such confidence in her, that, when she becomes a widow, the right of guardianship of the children is vested in her, — a situation greatly superior to that of the English or even the American wife.

She has the largest share in the education of the children. In constant intercourse with them, shielding them with the utmost solicitude, the better to gain their confidence, she guides them without her hand being seen. And, if any grief or any chagrin saddens their young life, it is in her bosom that they come to pour out their sorrows, and receive most soothing sympathy. In all these relations, the heart plays a great part, even when the husband participates. Perhaps this sort of education leaves something to be desired for the better tempering of the child's disposition. As to the husband, his *role* commences later, when labor and trials in common finally bring him in closer relation with his son.

If we look at the wife herself, in relation to her brothers and sisters, we shall find that the most perfect equality governs their right of inheritance from father or mother; and, if these latter desire to disregard this equality, or favor a third party to the prejudice of their children, the law fixes the limits of this power of disposal. It is a protection afforded to all without distinction.

VI.

Position in Society.

With our French habits, the wife is the natural centre, not only around whom the family is grouped, but also as an object of attraction for society. In all the epochs of our history, she has greatly contributed to the refinement of manners. In the seventeenth and eighteenth centuries, and during our times, have there not been seen many women gathering around them all the wits *d'élite*, all the men of any mark, whom they possessed the secret of drawing together by that irresistible power which we yield to without feeling, the success of which is so often but dependent upon a happy word kindly said, always meeting some weakness of our nature, of which they have such wonderful perception?

VII.

Participation in Business.

But the prerogatives of the French married woman do not exist alone in the family and society. She can engage in the same spheres of activity as her husband, — the career of business, of commerce, or of industry is open to her : and she has shown the same aptitude in each as he. This is very different from the condition of woman among the Romans, for, married or not, she was condemned to a perpetual guardianship, caused by her frivolity of character. The English, like the Americans, seem to have taken the Romans as models on this point. I do not think that such freedom is granted the married woman in any country as in France. And the Americans might well imitate us ; for, democratic people as they are, they lavish a thousand marks of deference upon woman, and yet hold her in complete guardianship.

VIII.

Marriage Considered as an Element of Population.

The principal, and that which should be the sole, agent in the increase of population is marriage. Hence, aside from individual interests, all nations have honored, sustained, and encouraged it in every way. The celibate who checks its progress has always been regarded with an evil eye, except, perhaps, since the appearance of Christianity, in accordance with which he has shown his reason for so remaining.

Marriage is an element of wealth for a country, from the family of which it is the source. And if that was considered the only sign of prosperity, then France would be much behind England, and far in the rear of the United States. The last two censuses* have shown that the increase of population in France for the preceding ten years has been very slow, and less than we should have the right to expect in a country in perfect peace, where emigration is but slight. Should this result be attributed to a great increase of celibacy, or a transference of

* Moniteur, Dec. 31, 1856; and Journal des Economists, February, 1857, p. 225.

the habits of celibacy to marriage? Both causes
may unite to produce it.

This result is a subject of regret, even alarm,
to the economists. Some of them, in the
tumult of their apprehensions, would almost
see revived the law of Pappia Poppea, which
made an era in the reign of Augustus and
Roman legislation, and which, at the same time
that it punished the celibate, encouraged fecun-
dity in a thousand ways. Others, less radical,
would only re-establish the edict of 1666, by
which Louis IV. granted certain pensions to
parents of ten children, with an increase for
those who had twelve or more. But these ideas
have had their day. They testify to the blind
despotism that believes possible what it wishes.
As an ecclesiastical historian* has said, " as if
the multiplication of the human species could
be affected by our interference, when we see
that the number increases and decreases in
accordance with the will of Providence." Every
nation that has attempted to regulate this subject has soon found the futility of its interference; and we must remember that the only
thing requisite is to improve morality, and render life more simple, in order to restore to marriage all its charms and its natural fruitfulness.

* Sozomène, liv. i. chap. ix.

CHAPTER II.

MARRIAGE IN ENGLAND.

I.

Preliminaries.

In England we have an anticipation of the practice of marriage in the United States, as respects the great freedom left to young girls in exercising their choice. There are, nevertheless, very marked differences. One of the prominent features in England is the paternal authority, which governs the acts of the family, and is an object of respect for all. A single word shows this. When a son addresses his father, he does not say " father," but " sir." To take this literally would, however, be attaching too great importance to it; for filial affection may be readily reconciled with paternal authority. Our old-fashioned French manners would bear witness to this. It is, however, an affection

restrained, and its exhibition moderated by
respect. On the other hand, both parents in
return for this deference, allow their children
great freedom in all that concerns marriage. A
young English girl may make her choice, without being either guided or restrained ; she generally, however, does it under the eyes of her
mother, who, except under peculiar and grave
circumstances, allows the attachment of her
daughter to arise and grow up for the person
she desires to marry.

In a country like this, a great centre of commerce, industry, and business of all kinds,
where any one may, by his perseverance, intelligence, and activity, attain a certain degree of
fortune, the dowry of the young lady is less a
matter of importance than her personal qualities and the position of her family. It is different in France, where a large number of men, in
civil or military office, having fixed and very
moderate salaries, are so placed as to be obliged
to yield to pecuniary considerations. It must,
moreover, be remembered that of later years the
old-fashioned disinterestedness in the business
of marriage has gradually been changing in
England, as elsewhere. It is the re-actionary
tendency of the century felt everywhere.

However this may be, the young English girl

is, so far as her parents are concerned, quite free from any restraint upon her choice. Moreover, marriage is not so premature as in France ; time is given for the judgment to be formed and matured. Reason subdues the impulses so natural at this age and under such circumstances.

Yet one thing serves sometimes to mislead these young hearts. English life is wholly domestic, and contact with the world is often quite limited. Moreover, the immense possessions of England in every latitude, and her great marine interests, take from the domestic circle a considerable number of men who are still young ; whence results a large disproportion between the sexes. The circle from which young girls can make their choice is very limited, and they often may not find there the man with whom they would unite their destiny. In the hope of better opportunity, many English families frequent the sea-side watering-places and Baths, or journey about ; and thus in this atmosphere, not always the most pure, a certain number of marriages take their origin. Here, in this artificial life, marriage is urged on, and, the mask often mistaken for the natural face, fashion helps it forward, the young girl's judgment is blinded, and her selection is left to all the hazard of a single meeting. When the choice is made, it must be sacredly kept.   Here commences the *role* of the law.

II.

Celebration of Marriage in England.

In olden time the validity of a marriage in England was questioned, when a minister of the established religion was not present; but, for a long time, his presence has only been considered a matter of conscience, and not of necessity. Moreover, the consent of the father, mother, or guardian, as well as the publication of the banns, were not indispensable. No particular form was necessary; and when, later, under the action of Lord Hardwicke's statute, certain formalities were made imperative, the nullity of a marriage could not be obtained on the ground of absence of prescribed formalities, unless this nullity was declared as sanctioned. The consequences of such imperfect laws could not but be soon seen, and reformation was attempted.

The last statute regulating this matter dates from the reign of William the Fourth. He established registrars of districts, who kept a register, in which parties desiring to marry recorded notice of their intention, with details necessary to inform those who might be interested in opposing it. This register was open and free to the public. After twenty-one days of this sort of publication, the registrar granted a license ; that is to say, a certificate stating that there was no opposition to the marriage, and that it might be proceeded with. If opposition was made, the registrar had the right to inquire and see if there was foundation for it ; and, in case of doubt, it was referred to the registrar-general, who made final decision.

These formalities complied with, the marriage could be performed by a minister of the established church of England, according to the rites peculiar to it, or by the rabbi for the Jews, or by an elder for the Quakers, or by the registrar for any of these. The ceremony must take place in the registrar's office, between eight and twelve o'clock in the morning, in the presence of witnesses ; the parties declaring under oath, in the contract, that they did not know any cause why the marriage should not be celebrated.

III.

Gretna Green.

To avoid these restrictions, the English very often escaped over the boundary, to Scotland. — where the laws on this point are very different, — and by the blacksmith of Gretna Green were quickly married, without formality or obstacle. But a bill, which passed Parliament, Dec. 31, 1856, declares, henceforth, such irregular marriages of the English in Scotland not valid in England, unless one of the parties at the time of marriage is a resident of Scotland, or has lived there twenty-one days previously.

Thus we see that a certain amount of formality is required of persons in England who are about to marry, but that the door of Scotland is always open for those who desire to avoid it. The one and twenty days' residence in the latter country is easily avoided by a subsequent short absence, or by complacent witnesses, so that the only barrier raised by the law is broken through. It is remarkable that in England, where the paternal will is received as a dogma in the family, the father's or the mother's consent is not required; and the large number of marriages which take place at Gretna Green proves that their assent is far from being always obtained, which is equivalent to saying that their authority is very often unrecognized. This peculiar trait in manners is not new : it seems to be even traditional, if we may believe Montesquieu, who states that in his time in England, "the young girls often abuse the law, to marry of their own choice, without consulting their parents."*

IV.

Marriage in Scotland.

The law in Scotland, which in certain respects seems made to keep up the separation of the two countries, requires no other formality than the publication of the banns in the parish where the parties reside. And a minister of any denomination is authorized to perform the marriage, with no other requisition than the consent of the parties desiring to be united. Justices of the peace cannot perform the rite ; but they can give a certificate of the wish expressed in their presence, and this is sufficient to render the marriage valid.

* Esprit des Lois, vol. iii., p. 428.

Such is the substance of the law on this matter in England and Scotland.

V.

Position of the English Wife.

Let us look at the position of the English wife, in the family, in society, and in the eye of the law.

In England, the married woman is only the equal of her husband in a religious point of view, not otherwise. She is, it is true, the object of his affections and regards, but it cannot be said that she is really his companion, the confidante of his inmost thoughts ; for the Englishman does not disclose them to his wife. This is not a want of confidence in her ; it belongs to the national character, and to the consciousness every man has of his own personal dignity and superiority to his wife, which public opinion and the law accord him under all circumstances. And, as everything in society is controlled by a sort of code of decorum, custom is busied with the regulation of relations which amongst other people are left to mutual affection, and by it alone guided.

The mother in England is, it is true, the centre of the family, around whom are grouped the
husband and children ; all are strongly bound
together, yet they cannot be said to be united.
Each has a marked out and defined position.
There is a blending of deference and independence, constituting one of the characteristic
traits of the English family, which is very striking to the French, among whom the family circle has a very different aspect of freedom, distinctions being less marked, but not on that
account forgotten. Nevertheless, it may be,
that, in contrasting and comparing the two systems, we come to the conclusion that it would
be better to modify both, by lessening the for-
malism of one, and the too great freedom of the
other.

VI.

The Domestic Hearth turned into a Boarding-House.

English domestic life, the *home*, otherwise
so commended and estimable, has for some
time past been changing greatly among the
mercantile class, especially of the larger cities.
The expense of living, luxury, and a multitude

of new wants, press heavily on the limited
resources of a large number of the people.
These exigencies must be met; and, to satisfy
them, recourse is had to means totally at variance with English manners and with tradition,
which is, notwithstanding, so powerful in this
country.   I speak of the custom that has
grown up of taking *pensionnaires*, — what in
English is called keeping a boarding-house.
Thus, for example, in London and the neighborhood, many families resort to this expedient; and
fill the papers with their advertisements to the
public, especially to the unmarried.

This new element introduced into the domestic circle, often without much circumspection or
precaution, renders the family relations more
free, and sometimes compromises them.   It is
the life in common, with all its hazards, substituted for the retired home one ; and we may
readily foresee the evils arising from it. At first,
excused by real, even absolute, necessity, this
mode of life has by interested persons finally
been employed for abominable purposes. Absolutely snares set for the good-nature and credu-
lity of the public. A direct influence is brought
to bear upon the weaknesses of a boarder, to
entice him to commit some offence, which has
been meanly watched, and for which he is to be

made to pay dearly. This custom has been
sketched by the masterly hand of Dickens, in
his story of Pickwick ; but the picture he drew
did not permit him to expose all the peculiarities of this mercantile strategy, notwithstanding
their interest.   From a reserve which the reader
will appreciate, I shall abstain also.

VII.

Society Life.

English life is generally domestic ; society,
in our sense of the word, does not exist in
England, except perhaps in some aristocratic
salons in London.   A few distinguished women
may be found there, but they appear rather as
meteors than constellations.   It is not from lack
of talent, but the field for it, — a vital difference in the organization of French and English
society.   In a social point of view it is a means
of influence now lost to the English woman,
leaving much to be desired in this country, and
its development is, moreover, checked by the
feeling of rank so strongly rooted in the upper
classes.

VIII.

Civil Rights of the English Woman.

In civil life, the English married woman is quite ignored. By the Marriage Act, her husband becomes the proprietor of her personal property, and has the interest of her real estate. He is her legal guardian ; and, when by agreement matters are arranged differently, trustees are appointed, who have charge and control of her property, — in which case she and her husband are dependent upon their probity and intelligence, they having the power to misuse or mismanage it, not to speak of the disputes which may arise between them and the husband with regard to the better disposal of the wife's estate. All this form reminds us of the customs of a bygone age, based on the legal presumption that the wife was incapable of taking care of her own interests. I will not speak of the other circumstances in which the law takes for granted the incapacity of the wife, and her inferiority to the husband. It is the peculiar trait alone which I wish to point out, without entering into technical details.

We can understand why, in the face of a law so unjust, English women, even those unmarried, should not, like the French under certain circumstances, desire to enter the sphere of business or industry. They would fail, certainly not from a lack of intelligence, but because confidence and credit were withheld from them. Whatever opposes opinion or prejudice must expect certain failure.

IX.

The English Woman considered as an Heir.

As an heir, the English woman's position is not less subordinate. She must yield to considerations of policy or to aristocratic tendencies, which influence the middling classes, who also desire to keep up primogeniture. The greater part of the land, being held by the nobility, falls by entail to the eldest son of each family. The daughters have a share in the division of the other property. But, very often, their portion is singularly reduced by a will; which may even entirely set them aside, in virtue of the power granted without reserve to the father of the family. Hence the daughters are often completely sacrificed; and fall from the state of opulence, in which they were educated, to a position almost of dependence. This great inequality between the daughters and their eldest brother affects the family feeling, under any circumstances ; for it tends to separate more and more the different members from each other. The younger brothers, if they are as badly treated as their sisters, have at least the resource of following some career which may lead them to a fortune, and so repair the injustice of the law. But the woman is by custom condemned to a position of helplessness, which really renders her worse off than any of her brothers.

X.

Divorce, and Separation from Bed and Board, in England.

If, passing by all general considerations, we look at the miseries of an ill-assorted marriage, it is then that the English woman is truly worthy of sympathy. According to the old law, which was in force till 1856, a wife who was abandoned by her husband could not keep the earnings of her labor, or the assistance received from her family. What complaints and what sufferings remained so long without redress ! Meantime, a necessity of radically altering the law of divorce induced Parliament occasionally to interest itself in the fate of the deserted wife.

By the Bill of Reform of 1857, every woman, deserted by her husband, can withhold from him and his creditors all she can acquire by her industry, and that which she may inherit, or have willed to her. She has the power to dispose of her property, and to proceed at law for the preservation and maintenance of her rights, as though she were not married ; and, finally, to give married women of all classes the benefit of these new provisions, magistrates of the metropolitan police in London, and justices of the peace in the counties, are invested with the right of granting this sort of emancipation, when they find it sufficiently justified.

This is a great innovation in English law. It is a provision truly extravagant in the eyes of the most liberal legislator ; for it destroys the marital control, while leaving the conjugal knot still tied. It does more than protect the wife against her husband ; it overshoots the mark, by leaving her without protection from *herself*, since it allows her to dispose of any future fortune, even patrimony, which she may receive. It is falling from one extreme into the opposite. Such, however, is the general tendency of law made now-a-days.

Divorce has existed a long time in England ; but, until the Bill of Reform of which I have spoken, this legal redress has only been accessible to the wealthy. It was, in fact, a law of distinction. The inextricable labyrinth of procedures, their injustice, the exclusive jurisdictions, and the enormous costs, all rendered an appeal to the law impossible,— at least for the large majority. Hence followed second marriages, without the first being broken by divorce ; moreover, adulteries, and illegitimate births. They shut their eyes to the crime of polygamy, although it was declared a felony. Facts had a power the penal law could not repress. The latter was forced to retreat. The evil acquired such proportions, that Parliament interested itself, and totally changed the law, by substituting an entirely new state of things, which is being tried now, and which may be summed up as follows :

A husband can claim a divorce from his wife solely on the ground of adultery ; she, on the contrary, is obliged to prove more against her husband, to obtain a dissolution of the bond. Not only must he have been guilty of the crime, but his accomplice must be a woman whom he would not have the right to espouse, were he free, on account of legal prohibition, from consanguinity or affinity ; or he must, by marrying

his accomplice, have thereby committed bigamy ; or else there must, besides the commission
of the deed, be some cruelty on the part of the
husband towards his wife, or abandonment for
two years or more without valid excuse. The
wife can, besides, claim two other causes for
divorce ; thus, she can take advantage of her
husband's having been guilty of rape, or by
some unnatural crime rendered himself amenable to the law. To claim these rights, however,
there must be nothing in the conduct of the one
appealing, to extenuate the fault of the other.
And it lies with the court to decide under these
circumstances. In the place of the special jurisdictions for which these sort of affairs were formerly reserved, a court has been substituted
composed of judges detached from the other
courts ; and the procedures and costs have been
so modified and reduced as to render this tribunal accessible to all, or at least the majority.

Divorce being naturally so extreme a measure,
endeavor has been made to induce the married
couple, under certain circumstances, to accept
an expedient, which, not being equivalent to a
divorce, does not shut the door to future recon-
ciliation. Separation from bed and board (*separation de corps*) has been introduced, which
does not dissolve the marriage bond, but simply

loosens it. This may be claimed, 1st, In case of abandonment of either party, for two years or more ; 2d, For adultery ; and 3d, For ill usage so severe as to cause fear of life. Jurisdiction in affairs of this sort is invested in courts of justice, with trial by jury.

This law, so suddenly and totally altered, has revealed one of the weaknesses of English society. In reality, statistics have shown that since the establishment of this new jurisdiction, the number of applications for divorce has increased beyond all expectation ; so that the court cannot get through with the business before it under three years. Good people now think that they have gone too far on this road of reform, — it is so difficult in experimenting upon the body politic, as upon individuals, to find a remedy adapted to the complaint, and not exceed the dose which can be borne !

CHAPTER III.

MARRIAGE IN AMERICA.

I.

Preliminaries.

I COME now to marriage in America.
The young American enjoys still greater freedom than the English girl ; for she has the independence of race, and that coming from tradition, increased by contact with democratic manners. It is, however, but fair to remember, that
this liberty and independence do not have the
same inconveniences, and do not present the
same dangers as they would elsewhere ; for, in
America, woman is under the shield of public
opinion, and this is no unmeaning word. However inexperienced in life, she may travel alone,
and pass through the whole United States without a man daring to hazard a word or gesture
in her presence which could offend her. She

is, moreover, the object of every attention and regard. This deference does great honor to the intelligence of the Americans, who have realized in the midst of the *pêle-mêle* of democratic life, that woman ought to be placed above the general level ; and yet nothing in this affects the idea of equality, since she remains a stranger to the struggles of active life.

The young American girls very early take part in the reunions of which they, together with the young men of their own age, form, either exclusively, or nearly so, the nucleus ; thus leaving out those whom marriage has already received under its banner. It has been very wittily said of some of these reunions, that the cradles are the only things lacking. Here and there we meet with *esprit*, but what one mostly hears is a certain small talk that aims less at wit than mere sound. If done privately, it becomes what in English is called flirtation. It is as it were a tilt of desultory remarks without apparent signification, but whose intended aim is always marriage, without the episodes formed by preparatory incidents. Interest will be found more or less at the bottom of every one's thoughts. And how can it be otherwise where the young girls know that they must depend upon *themselves* to find a husband ?

But, if we often can but see in these reunions a sort of *champ d'affaires*, we must needs
recognize the true and deep affections which
grow up in the midst of these frivolities, where
the heart has staked much, and not weighed
obstacles. Suddenly, unforeseen circumstances
arise which prevent the projected union taking
place. The young girl, unaccustomed to meet
with restraint, is crushed by this resistance that
is stronger than she. Sometimes she succumbs
to it ; and, if she survives the misfortune, what
ravages do we not see in her feelings, spirits,
and heart ! There remains only perfect indifference to life, and bitter scorn for society. An
unfortunate, whom a more carefully directed
education, a more foreseeing society, might, no
doubt, have saved from such danger.

Besides these reunions, it is, as in England, at
the Springs, at watering-places, and in travelling,
that the young American girl seeks a husband ;
and, when she thinks the occasion favorable,
engages in this search alone, without the advice
of those who by nature and affection are placed
at her side as her most intimate and devoted
advisers. When still quite young, ignorant of
herself, life not yet a lesson, when circumstances
the most frivolous, appearances the most decep-
tive, and errors of judgment, may blind her

reason, — she makes the most important decision of her life.

Independent by nature and education, she
feels less than we can realize of the hesitation
which is a part of the character of the young
French girl.   She is, moreover, naturally disposed to receive with the greatest reluctance
any opposition on the part of her parents ; and,
with certain exceptions, rarely met with outside
of families where tradition has been more a precept, this delicate deference of a daughter to her
mother is not seen, — in reality, the most touching homage which can be offered the parent to
whom all is owed.

It is under these conditions that marriage is
very often formed and contracted in the United
States.   We can understand the law not being
more exacting than custom, and therefore not
requiring the consent of the parents to their
children's marriage.   Consent is in fact nearly
always given.   But it would be very curious to
inquire and ascertain, as a trait of manners, how
often this consent is not obtained, except too
late, in order to satisfy public opinion.   We have
seen that the number of English marriages made
at Gretna Green reached so high a figure that
Parliament interested itself, and endeavored to
find a remedy ; but no such provision exists for

the United States, except, perhaps, in reference to elopements, of which I shall hereafter speak.

II.

Civil Capacity for Marriage. — Celebration.

In the United States, following the Common Law of England, which is the general rule, — modified, however, in some of the States, — the minimum age for marriage is fourteen years for the man, and twelve for the woman. Having passed this age, the young people can dispense with the consent of their father, mother, and guardian. It is also true, that, according to this same law, the marriage contract can be entered into, with the consent of the father and mother, at seven years of age. But it does not seem that parents could be so unnatural as to promote such unions, — except, perhaps, under pretence of betrothing.

Just as the consent of the parents is not required, so the Common Law does not compel the publication of the banns, or require witnesses to the act, or even the signatures of the parties ; and the marriage may be performed by a justice of the peace, or a minister of religion,— no matter

where they may reside, even outside of the community of the espoused's home, — at any hour, and
in any place.   What a departure from the manners of the Pilgrims !   No more paternal authority ; clandestinity is substituted in broad daylight,
— the salutary participation of a minister of religion often set aside, and his place filled by the
presence of some obscure justice of the peace,
or other subordinate officer, unknown to all parties !   These customs are fortunately not yet very
widely spread : but it is a great defect in the
law, to deprive marriage of a certain solemnity,
which renders its importance better understood ;
and to remove from it the guaranty of publicity,
which keeps alive the respect of mankind, and
from which only too many people seek to escape.

It is true, some people hold that the publicity
of marriage is of no interest ; that the union of
the individuals is their exclusive affair alone, and
concerns no one else.   This reasoning arises
from the predominant idea in America, that the
individual is superior to the community, and
that the latter should not exercise any restraints,
except in rare cases, and from reasons of most
serious moment.   But it is forgotten that marriage is the foundation of the family, and creates
new relations between persons who have been
strangers to each other ; and hence come rights

and duties of every nature, domestic, civil, political : and we cannot too much protect an institution, the most ancient and respectable of all,
where morality is tempered by social condition.

These ideas, however, seem to have made
some impression upon certain minds ; for, I
believe, there are two States where the guaranty
of publicity is required, but without penal enforce-
ment. It should be stated, that, in the United
States as in England, the fact of cohabitation
suffices to render the judges very lenient in
making valid an imperfect marriage. Probably,
it was with this idea that the Court of the
Queen's Bench, the highest in England, decided,
in 1855, that a Protestant minister could perform his own marriage ceremony ; and, on this
ground, declared valid one which had taken
place under these conditions. In France, such
principles are in opposition to our most elementary ideas of right ; and nothing could be urged
less likely to admit the possible application of
similar theories than the consideration that the
act had been accomplished.

III.

Eccentric Forms of Celebration.

Circumstances often unite in giving the celebration of certain unions a *bizarre* appearance.
Thus it is related, that, in the State of Maine,
the conductor of a railroad train, who, no doubt,
was too much occupied to give a day to his
marriage, invited his *fiancée* and a minister into
a car ; and, while the train was in motion, the
marriage ceremony was performed.   So that the
man started from one station a bachelor, and
arrived married at the next.   It is but one of
the thousand examples of life as it goes in this
fast country.

A still more original marriage is that of two
young *fiancés* in Virginia, who, in 1855, had to
cross a river in search of the minister who was
to unite them : it was so swollen that the passage was impossible, so the young people
called to the first person who appeared on the
opposite bank, and explained the object of their
pursuit.   The pastor came ; the paper which
contained the necessary permission was rolled
up, attached to a stone, and thrown across to
the minister, who, after reading it, and going

through with the usual questions and responses, across the stream, married the couple according to the rites of the church. Peculiar as these marriages appear in form, they are none the less real, and have all the legal consequences.

IV.

Mock Marriages.

The two facts which have just been narrated, are only peculiar so far as the form is concerned ; but there are others which seriously injure the respect due to marriage, and the law which protects it. An American author* has well said, "Among the follies which certain people give themselves to are mock marriages, made for amusement." According to this writer, if two people, not having the serious intention of marrying, nevertheless, go through with the formalities, for excitement or amusement, they are none the less united by a legal bond, which prevents their contracting another union while this exists. This is precisely what happened in Pennsylvania, in 1857. A certain Miss J. was at

* Bishop, On Marriage and Divorce, § 83.

a party with Mr. B. ; and, jesting about marriage, they imitated what takes place under such circumstances. Mr. B. asked the hand of Miss J., who consented. To continue the pleasantry, they went before the pastor of the neighborhood, and the conjugal knot was tied. Meantime the young lady, after recovering her presence of mind, would not carry on the counterfeit marriage. But the husband took the thing in earnest, and claimed the execution of the union. The wife refused ; and was obliged, in order to free herself from the legal consequences of her thoughtless engagement, to make application for a divorce. The author of whom I speak cites another instance very analogous, and in this case, as in the former, a divorce was granted. If the law was more foreseeing and really protective, such scandals would not take place, and the respect which ought to surround marriage would be preserved.

V.

Forced Marriages.

It is a wonder that matters of this kind are not more frequent ; for, according to the doctrine adopted by the different courts, circumstantial evidence alone may prove the fact of an engagement to marry. "It is not necessary," said a judge to the jury, in the State of New York, "that a promise of marriage should be made in· express terms; frequent visits, conversation aside, expressions of attachment, some presents offered, walks taken together, etc., are sufficient circumstances on which to rely in proving the existence of a marriage engagement. And, if this evidence is such as to convince the judge, the law does not require anything more to prove the tie."

This arbitrary interpretation, in a matter so grave, has opened the door to the most shameful speculations. Marriageable girls and widows, repudiating the reserve which belongs to their sex, set themselves in pursuit of wealthy men, always those advanced in life ; and seek, by artifices more or less ingenious, to attract them to themselves ; and so, by some familiarities, in which they always take the initiative, to give rise to the idea with the public, that a marriage would follow. And, when they think sufficient evidence has been accumulated, raising the mask, they demand either marriage or a heavy indemnity. Sometimes to escape scandal, even unmerited, this Machiavelian pressure is yielded to ; and a sum, generally pretty heavy, is sacrificed to obtain peace. If the demand is resisted, the affair is quickly laid before the court, and the jury decides.

In these questions, which touch prejudices, preconceived opinions, and envy, — the special enemy of a wealthy man, — the jury is easily impressed by the appeal of the woman who appears as a victim ; and we see verdicts so exaggerated as to be rather impulses *ab irato* than judicial decisions.

Quite recently, a case of this kind occurred in the State of Missouri ; and the jury, yielding I know not to what impulse, condemned a wealthy man of the place, sued simply on presumption, to pay $100,000 damage to a woman who kept a lodging-house in St. Louis. The victim of this swindle, not submitting to the decision, made appeal ; and judges, more calm, and better informed of the precedents of the woman, annulled the verdict, releasing the accused from further prosecution.

An American journal,* moderate in its opinions, and holding considerable influence, accompanies the narration of this trial with the following remarks :

* New York Semi-weekly Times, April 6, 1860.

"It is time such a lesson was taught [these sort of women]; for suits for breach of promise of marriage have become disgustingly common throughout the United States. Half a dozen heavy damages seem to have stimulated the appetite of a certain number of women, more or less young, and excited them on all sides to commence prosecutions. It has become absolutely dangerous for wealthy men to be polite towards an unmarried woman! We believe they will now be able to breathe a little more freely."

This is a trait in morals, of English importation, nearly unknown among us. Let us hope to escape the contagion.

What strange law! If it concerns the sale of the smallest corner of land, there must be a deed signed, sealed in the presence of witnesses, and recorded in a register. If it is a will, still more is demanded. But, for the most important act of life, the simplest tokens are sufficient to prove the existence of an engagement between the parties. As if marriage did not involve consequences of fortune more important than a sale or a will! In view of this excessive readiness of the law in the formation of marriage, should we not be authorized in saying that it aimed only at a promiscuous intercourse, designed to increase the population, without regard to moral considerations, or the future of the family? This idea is still further strengthened, by the corresponding facilities afforded for divorce, as we shall hereafter see.

VI.

Marriages in the West.

One of the causes which contribute to give great impulse to sudden and inconsiderate marriages is the rapid development of the new States of the Union, where a large number of adventurers flock to seek their fortune, meeting with greater or less prosperity. They at first form only settlements of men ; but, with money, the desire for family makes itself felt, and many young girls, who have some education, seek a husband there, — not from motives of affection, but impelled by ambition and the thirst for novelty, which incites them to tempt the chances of these alliances.

The settlements in the West are so primitive, there is so little civilization, that a peculiar stamp is impressed upon them, which is attractive. Circumstances, however, sometimes prevent the immigration of women, and the gloom and languor which pervade these sections can scarcely be imagined. Thus, in some of the rapidly formed territories, we may perhaps find only men, — it having chanced that women had not thought to go in this direction. We soon find appearing in the papers positive supplications from these unfortunate men to the young women of the other States, entreating them to come, and share their life, giving them their choice, and promising dowries quite comfortable and well assured. In good time, an echo is heard to this request; the desired helpmates arrive, and soon the country beams with happiness and prosperity, — a result that money alone would have been powerless to produce.

The scarcity of women always makes itself heard at intervals in the regions of the West. Thus, we find, in May, 1857, a newspaper of Iowa, the Iowa Reporter, making a most energetic appeal to the women of all lands to flock there. It says that the last census, taken in June, 1856, shows that the excess of the male population in Iowa is thirty-three thousand six hundred and forty, without counting the immigrants who have arrived since then (nearly a year), and those who are yet expected. It finishes by stating, "We are sixty thousand short of women to make the balance equal!" Is there not in this formidable number a lamentation fitted to touch the hearts of the most indif-

ferent! There are some women who emigrate
to these countries, like those who go to the
English colonies in India, sure, no matter what
their position, of being eagerly sought after upon
their arrival. What takes place in the West,
however, is merely a transitory condition, and
cannot serve as the basis for judgment in general.

VII.

Misalliances.

We might suppose that the great liberty
granted to young girls, in America, would cause
them to feel the responsibility which their decision involved ; and, in doing an act of freewill,
they would not offend any social proprieties.
But it is not always so. Misalliances now and
then take place, which simple self-respect would
forbid, and yet which do occur, to the great
injury of the domestic circle and public morality.
Even in the heart of republics, there are inev-
itable inequalities of position. These do not
result from birth, but from education. And, if
this is true of the relations of man to man, how
much greater must be this inequality between

men and women! It would seem as if the delicacy of their nature, perfected by education, ought to form an impassable abyss between the latter and a coarse and vulgar man, — above all as respects marriage. The exceptions which sometimes occur to this natural law must therefore be regarded as deviations. Unfortunately, they are found in the United States, as we have also seen, quite recently, in France ; and, in citing two cases only of this kind, it is to prove that even in the country where the family seems best protected by public opinion, there is no exemption from these domestic evils. The two cases of which I speak are similar, although there was no connection between them. They were the marriages, in 1857, of two young persons belonging to wealthy families of New York and Boston respectively. Yielding — I know not to what infatuation, they eloped with men of low condition, whom they afterwards married. One of them chose her father's coachman, the other the coachman of a friend of the family.* The marriages were, most unfortunately, legal ; and the parents, although totally opposed to such alliances, were obliged to submit to these calamities, which they could not avert. Such unions

---

* Boston News Letter, Sept. 12, 1857; and Semi-weekly Tribune, 1857.

are branded by public opinion in America ; but could not the mother have prevented them by a more vigilant solicitude ?

VIII.

Forced Marriages. — Elopements.

There are other cases where social propriety, though not so rudely shocked, yet has claims which the parents would not see disregarded. One cause of these is the great negligence of mothers in allowing their daughters to remain alone with some teacher of accomplishments, — confidence being reposed in the latter, not in view of his character, but from the art which he teaches ; and, moreover, it must be said, in order to escape an hour of monotonous surveillance. In this intimate intercourse, where the teacher seeks to awaken in his pupil the sense of the beautiful, to develop her taste, her natural talent, it is so easy to make an indirect appeal to the heart, to vanity, or to weaknesses of any kind ! The language which gives to the art itself a seductive fascination, and which he uses as no other, acts as a dissolvent upon the purity of the scholar, and sometimes leads her into error. In such case, as whenever there is too great clashing, the parents set themselves in opposition to their daughter, nearly always too late, however ; and, if this resistance does not soon cease, an elopement follows.

This sort of scandal is rare, but not perhaps sufficiently so, — proof of which may be found in the newspapers of every State. One of these has said, "The mania for elopements has become intermittent, — sometimes, like a passing epidemic, there seeming to be seasons when it is more severe."

The regretable fact is, however, that often there is no real pretext for these elopements. Sometimes only a little more forbearance, a little more entreaty, is needed to obtain the consent of the parents. A refusal is not waited for, a request for assent is not even hazarded, and the elopement takes place. It is an eccentricity which seems to give character to the young girl who yields to it, and to make her the fashion. In this commonplace life, where each day is like the one which has passed and the one to succeed, and where amusements are few, we can imagine some natures would feel they might live better by shaking off this oppressive atmosphere which surrounds them, by soaring up into regions inaccessible to the vulgar, where they may blos-

som out ; but, from whence, they quickly fall back
into prosaic reality.   In all this, there is no room
for affection or freedom of action.   It is a mere
whim, a caprice, which has sacrificed honor, the
quiet of the family circle, and the whole future,
where a divorce often looms in the horizon.

As opinion has not the power to effectually
influence these habits, minds even the most
pure seem to become habituated to regarding
such occurrences mentioned as the simple acci-
dents of life, which time will perhaps some day
explain.   It is chance which finally decides the
morality of the act.   There is a story of a young
lady, well brought up, and of excellent family,
whose sister had eloped with a wealthy gentleman.   The elopement was a complete success ;
and marriage following it was some consolation
for the parents.   As soon as the young sister
heard this good news, she went to tell it to a
lady of her acquaintance as a fortunate circumstance ; because it would make good a position
which had been compromised.   The lady remarked, that the result was a matter for congrat-
ulation, especially as the family and fortune of
the husband seemed to be suitable.   "See," she
added, "the danger of such situations."—"Ah!
yes," replied the young girl; "it does not always
turn out so well!"

What shocking *naïveté!*

I hasten to say that these eccentricities very rarely occur in the old families where we find good principles inculcated by the mother in her children, and which they hold as a precious heritage. But, in this country of marvels, so many new fortunes are suddenly made, that a vast field is open to all sorts of irregularities, even to those which should last cross the threshold of the home. Moreover, the foreign element which is gradually insinuating itself into American society does not contribute to refine it : quite the contrary ; and, if we may believe true and unprejudiced people, the nation has only swerved from the course which it held during the most brilliant period of its history, since foreign immigration has become so immense as to modify its civil and political condition.

IX.

Aristocratic Tendencies.

In opposition to these ill-assorted unions, which avowedly shock social propriety, must be mentioned one of the characteristic traits of the marrying disposition of the young American

girl. Her greatest ambition is to espouse a
man with a title. It is a weakness which affects
all classes, and to which everything is sacrificed.
An European having a noble title, doubtful perhaps, may go to the United States, and, no matter how little recommended, can be sure of
marrying wealth, after a short stay. It is sur-
prising to see the number of aristocratic buds,
and they are not always the best, on this repub-
lican shoot.

There are, undoubtedly, men of talent able
to uphold by their personal qualities the title
they have received from their ancestors, and
nothing is more praiseworthy than to seek their
alliance. That, however, is not generally the
first thought of the American girl. The *title*
is what she aspires to ; all else is of secondary
importance. Place before her two men, one of
whom has but his noble title ; and the other a
man distinguished in science, in letters, or in
business, — there will be no doubt of the young
American's choice. Her eyes are fixed beforehand on the wedding cards, where her title of
baroness, countess, or marquise will be spread
out for the first time in large letters. Her very
visiting cards will pay her homage each day;
moreover, to hear herself announced in salons
as a lady of rank will be a melody delicately

flattering to her vanity. And what renders it
more piquant is that her friends will congratulate themselves on the union as a conquest
made by their little circle, which will receive its
share of the ennoblement. We shall not find
here the solid basis of a democracy.

X.

The Law Favoring Fraud.

We have seen how improvident the law is
respecting guaranties for maintaining the true
character of marriage, causing the community to
give place to the individual, instead of combin-
ing these two interests for mutual advantage.
But a crime committed in New York in 1857
has rendered this truth prominent, by proving
not only that the law is improvident, but that it
is even an accomplice in great crimes. These
are the principal facts of the case :

A doctor by the name of Burdell lived in a
house belonging to him, in New York, a few
steps only from the most frequented thorough-
fare. His rooms were on the ground floor.
On the next story lived a woman by the name
of Cunningham, with whom it was claimed Bur-

dell had had a *liaison*. Several persons were in
the habit of visiting her, especially a man
named Eckel, who was supposed to have re-
placed Burdell in his intimacy. She had eagerly
and repeatedly urged the doctor to marry her,
but he had always refused. Meantime it was
said, that, as he was worth sixty or eighty thousand dollars, this woman Cunningham had
formed the design of murdering him, and,
probably, securing the right of succession. As
all which relates to the murder was not legally
proved, I can only repeat the facts as charged
by the accusation.

According to the accusation, the woman Cunningham went out one evening with a man, supposed to be Eckel, to the house of quite an
obscure Protestant minister, whom neither of
them knew. The man had a false beard, the
better to disguise himself; he gave his name as
Burdell; and they both requested to be united
in marriage. No other witness was present,
except a young daughter of the Cunningham
woman. The minister, without ascertaining the
identity of the parties, married them in a few
minutes, under the names which were told him.
No marriage contract was drawn up, and thus
no signatures given; in a word, no trace
remained of this guilty deed, except the cer-

tificate which the pretended married ones made the complaisant minister give them, attesting the performance of the ceremony. All this remained a secret in the house.

Two or three months afterwards, the City of New York was startled, as by a clap of thunder, at the news of the assassination of Burdell in his study, one night in the month of January. Upon the first suspicion, Eckel and the woman Cunninghan were arrested, and kept in secret confinement ; the proper investigations were instituted ; but no light was thrown upon the affair, and they were released and discharged.

If matters had rested here, the intent of the crime would not have been seen ; for the marriage would, at the most, have created a right of dower for this woman Cunningham, which was relatively of small importance. But the marriage was necessary, in order to feign a *grossesse* which would give an heir to the unfortunate Burdell. In reality, a *grossesse* was announced, and a false *accouchement* prepared. But, thanks to skilfully taken measures, the falseness of the *grossesse* and *accouchement* were established and legally proved ; so that the crime committed upon Burdell remained without result for its presumed authors.

Let us suppose, for a moment, that marriage

in America was surrounded by the same formalities and requirements as in France, then
certainly this assassination would have been
prevented. If there had been a required publication of the banns in an official bureau of the
parish ; if the identity of the parties must have
been assured ; if the ceremony must have been
authenticated by the presence of witnesses who
were of age and residents ; if its performance
had been required during the day, and not at
night, in a register's office ; if the signatures of
the parties and the witnesses were to have been
taken, and the marriage contract recorded in
the archives ; had all this been required, even
the thought itself of the crime would not have
arisen in the mind of whoever committed it.

XI.

Situation of the American Wife. — Revolt against the Laws of Marriage.

Not only the law which regulates the formation of marriage is faulty, but also that which
governs the relations and interests of the married between themselves. It is difficult to
explain the wife's passing suddenly and without
transition from a state of absolute independence

to one of complete dependence on her husband, and so legally incapacitated for civil rights as to place her nearly in the condition of minors, and those declared incapable of directing their own affairs. It is insulting the intelligence she was supposed to possess before marriage. We shall see, further on, what the civil incapacities are. This antiquated law comes from England, whence it was imported into the first colonies, and has there been preserved; as if with old, worn-out materials a new community could be built up, whose very spirit was in revolt against the causes which originated it! And such is the force of precedent, that the refinement of civilization has produced little, if any, modification in these laws.

The following are some of the most offensive points of the law:

1. The husband has ownership of all the personal property of the woman, at the time of marriage, unless special reservation has been made to prevent it.

2. The married woman cannot possess anything in her own name. Her property stands in the name of her husband, or in the hands of trustees.

3. All that she may earn by her industry belongs to her husband.

4. She cannot make a will.

5. At her death, her husband has the right of possession of her property; and other powers, greater than what the law grants her, in case of the husband's death, etc., etc.

The excessive privileges granted the latter are an anomaly in a democratic country. They cannot be justified by any plausible reasoning, except the force of tradition, — which influences, more than we think, the minds even of the most intelligent. Although some of the States have timidly entered upon the road of reform in this matter, the greater number oppose an invincible resistance to all innovation. Of this we can judge from two facts which I will now relate.

In 1857, the Legislature of Delaware was engaged with a motion to authorize married women holding property in their own name, without at all abridging the marital power. But the proposition was vigorously opposed, and finally defeated. It did not, it will be noticed, do anything more than bring the married woman into civil life, without giving her any power to make over property. The simple idea of change, however, prevented this just demand.

Here is another example, in one of the most advanced and intelligent States of the Union.*

In the session of 1857, the Legislature of

---

* Vide The Boston Post, April 28, 1857.

Massachusetts, sitting at Boston, was occupied
with a proposition, the object of which was to
grant a widow greater rights of survivorship
than then allowed by the law, so as to place her
upon nearly an equal footing with her husband,
when he outlived his wife. There was here no
excessive right or privilege, and yet this propo-
sal was violently opposed and defeated. One
of the senators maintained as a motive for his
opposition, that wives were already too much
inclined to disembarrass themselves of their
husbands, without our seeking to give more
stimulus to this desire. The senator made
allusion to certain crimes committed a short
time previously by wives upon their husbands,
— crimes which were imputed to a desire for
succession.

We can scarcely conceive such reasons having
weight with a legislative body, who ought to
regard things from a higher point of view. Such
crimes are only the very rarest exceptions. And
the charge cannot be exclusively brought against
women, for they are generally less open to considerations of interest than men.

This legislative opposition to claims, just and
moderate, excites a desire for reform ; and calls
forth rebellion against, and contempt for, the
law.

For some years past, there has been growing
up in the United States a phalanx of strong-
minded women, who hold that woman is as
trodden down there as in England ; and who
want to throw off this yoke, and obtain important changes of the law. To gain their ends,
they keep up discussion, hold meetings, write
in the papers, send petitions, even deputations,
to the legislatures. They appear before the
committees, and warmly defend the claims for
whose success they hope. Up to the present
time, their radical attempts have been defeated ;
but we may be assured, that, so long as they do
not obtain some signal result, the agitation will
continue. A single instance will show how far
the fanaticism of these reformers of the weaker
sex has gone.

One of them, a very intelligent woman, Miss
Lucy Stone, well known in Abolition circles,
married in May, 1855, in Massachusetts. She
espoused one of the leaders of this party. The
marriage was performed by the Rev. T. W. Hig-
ginson, of Worcester. In the contract, those
making it protest against the laws of the State
concerning marriage. This very curious protestation is thus expressed : *

---

* New York Tribune, Boston Traveller, May 4, 1855.

" While we acknowledge our mutual affection, by publicly assuming the sacred relationship of husband and wife, yet, in justice to ourselves and a great principle, we deem it a duty to declare, that this act on our part implies no sanction of, or promise of voluntary obedience to, such of the present laws of marriage as refuse to recognize the wife as an independent rational being, while they confer upon the husband an injurious and unnatural superiority, investing him with legal powers which no honorable man would exercise, and which no man should possess. We protest especially against the laws which give to the husband—

" 1. The custody of the wife's person.

" 2. The exclusive control and guardianship of their children.

" 3. The sole ownership of her personal, and use of her real estate, unless previously settled upon her ; or placed in the hands of trustees, as in the case of minors, lunatics, and idiots.

" 4. The absolute right in the product of her industry.

" 5. Also, against laws which give to the widower so much larger and more permanent an interest in the property of his deceased wife than they give to the widow in that of her deceased husband.

" 6. Finally, against the whole system by which 'the legal existence of the wife is suspended during marriage,' so that in most States she neither has a legal part in the choice of her residence, nor can she make a will, nor sue or be sued in her own name, nor inherit property.

" We believe that personal independence and equal human rights can never be forfeited, except for crime ; that marriage should be an equal and permanent partnership, and so recognized by law ; that, until it is recognized, married partners should provide against the radical injustice of present laws, by every means in their power.

"We believe, that, when domestic difficulties arise, no appeal should be made to existing tribunals ; but all difficulties should be submitted to the equitable adjustment of arbitrators, mutually chosen. Thus, reverencing law, we enter our earnest protest against rules and customs which are unworthy of the name, since they violate justice, — the essence of all law."

XII.

Protestation against the Law, by the Pastor who performs the Ceremony.

Setting aside the protestation which I have just transcribed, and taking into view only the grievances enumerated, one cannot but admit, that there are several which the Legislatures of all the States ought to redress, as being more in harmony with the spirit of the times, and also the customs of society in the United States. But what we cannot favor is the protestation itself. I know that this sort of protest is quite rare and very eccentric ; but it has and will have its imitators, especially in the Eastern States, where the desire for reform is almost an endemic malady. As a voucher for the extension of this spirit of resistance to the law, we have a letter to an editor of a newspaper, by the same minister who performed the marriage of Miss Stone, and which was published in a journal called the "Worcester Spy," edited in Massachusetts. This is the text:*

"I never perform the marriage ceremony, without a renewed sense of the iniquity of our present system of laws in respect to marriage, — a system by which man and wife are one, and that one is the husband. It was with my hearty concurrence, therefore, that the following protest was read and signed, as a part of the nuptial ceremony; and I send it to you that others may be induced to do likewise. T. W. H."

We cannot here in France understand this open opposition to the law, encouraged and sanctioned by the very person whose mission is to administer and defend it. We have too much respect for its authority not to obey it, till it is revoked. In the United States, individual freedom acts differently, and revolt against the law is not rare. Can we not say, with Lord Carlisle, "America is anarchy and a constable"?

* Boston Traveller and New York Tribune, May 4, 1855.

XIII.

Considerations of Inheritance. — The Rights of Women.

The Americans, while adopting the Common
Law of England, as the basis of their civil law,
have yet repudiated some provisions, as too
opposed to the spirit of their political institutions. Thus they have abolished the rights of
primogeniture, and all distinction between the
children of the two sexes relative to the division
of the inheritance from their parents. In this
respect, the American woman is more fortunate
than the English, receiving an equal share of
the paternal estate with her brothers.

It is true that the father or mother has the
right to dispose of all their fortune to the exclu-
sion of their children, or of openly favoring one
to the injury of the others, in unlimited disproportion ; but public opinion is so opposed to
everything of this kind, that it rarely happens
that parents make such dispositions, or that the
child, in whose favor they are made, takes
advantage of them. Would it not be better,
when a law is in opposition to public opinion,
to sacrifice it to the latter, rather than to tempt
human weakness to take advantage of it ?

But there is a dominant idea with the Americans, which greatly affects the force of these considerations. The lack of stability, which has till now prevented many fortunes from being built up, forces every one to see that he must be the maker of his own position, without counting too much upon the resources which his parents may leave him. Inheritances, that in France get the scandalous title of *les esperances*, are in the United States entirely consigned to future contingencies. Hence, few idle people are seen in this country. Each fills his own pocket, and appears satisfied in so doing. It is a real advantage which America has over France, where many young men of the upper classes, even of those who do not yet count a generation, refuse all honorable employment, and spend in advance their family patrimony; as if the dial hand to indicate the time of possession had moved too slowly.

We see from what has preceded, that, if the condition of the American woman leaves much to be desired in regard to her married position, this is not the case as respects her relation to her brothers, with whom she is on a perfect footing of equality.

XIV.

The Family and its Deviations in the North.

Now that we have seen how marriage is contracted, there remains to be stated what married life becomes.

The American, more especially the Yankee,*
brought up in the bosom of the family, appre-
ciates, while still young, the happiness of the
domestic circle ; he has contracted habits of
regularity, which wonderfully adapt him to wres-
tle with life.   He recognizes the sanctity of the
conjugal tie, early takes the obligation upon
himself, and does not refuse any of its duties.
Yet, although he does this, his wife is never the
confidante of his intimate and real thoughts.
With another, the heart will overflow under
grave and painful circumstances ; at home, it is
hermetically sealed.   Is it stoicism ?   No : he
is very impressible, and has little resignation.
Or is it not rather a mask, with which he covers
a real trouble that he would not have suspected.
His natural pride allows this supposition.   Having the greatest respect, in other things, for his

* This word Yankee is a corruption by the Indians of the French
word *Anglais.*

wife, he considers her less his companion, during prosperity and adversity, than as the preceptor of his children, and the one whom he loves best. He does not fail to render her marks of attachment, during the short time that he can spare from the affairs of the community, of the parish, of the county, of the State, or of the Union, and, most of all, his own personal business. His confidences are but the flitting incidents of his life; and, if we could read his thoughts, there would always be found a reserved corner for all kinds of speculations, — even in those moments when a man forgets himself.

The American wife is generally attached to her husband, — the father of her children. She devotes her care and attention to him. She is faithful; that is to say, she generally keeps the faith she has sworn. For this there are two causes: first of all, *principle;* then the quiet life she is so often obliged to lead. She devotes herself, above all, to the cares of the house; and the task is hard enough in a country where there is such independence, that the servant dismisses the master, and lets caprice get the better of duty. Moreover, this servant being almost always Irish, the antagonism of race is called forth, and the Celt takes a secret pleasure in obliging his American master to take *his* place, by quitting him abruptly.

This is one of the unpleasant sides of domestic life, which tends to compromise it, and cause it to lose all its advantages. And thus, to escape all these vexations, we see a certain number of families in the large cities installing themselves in the hotels or boarding-houses, — veritable caravansaries, where one lives somewhat *pêle-mêle*, with the appearance of luxury and show. It is a great trial for the wife. For, relieved of all occupation, she forgets the domestic life, contracts bad habits of thoughtlessness, sometimes dangerous *liaisons;* and the husband, as well as children, having no real centre for reunion, and separated moreover by this life of variety, withdraw themselves, with different purposes, till there is nothing left of the domestic circle but the name: its true meaning is completely lost. As to the married who have really a home, their life may be divided into two parts: the one passed during the winter in the city is truly the American home; but, in summer, things have quite another aspect.

A desire for going into the country has come into vogue, which tends to completely modify the family, nearly in the same way I have just spoken of. At the commencement of summer,

every lady wants to leave the city, and go to one
of the numerous and immense hotels that are to
be found at the seaside or the Springs, especially
where there is some particular attraction for visitors. Here every day is a round of dissipation
and festivity. Pride and folly call for lavish
expenditure. It is the "Vanity Fair" Thackeray
describes. This gay world, which renders every
one constantly conspicuous, is relished all the
more as the life in winter has been *triste* and
monotonous. The husband stays in the city to
attend to his business, or take part in politics;
and does not visit his wife, except at intervals,
— very much as a conservatory act to prevent
prescription. The children, brought up in the
midst of all this, especially the young girls, cannot regard life seriously, or appreciate the idea
of duty. Amusement is what attracts them;
and, in this general excitement, young people
busy themselves only with extravagance, parties,
and flirtation. The young men easily fall into
bad habits, the most frequent of which is drink-
ing to excess.

XV.

Domestic Life in the South.

Home life in the South is modified by the
service being performed by the slaves, whose
sudden quitting is not feared.   There is no need
of having recourse to hotel life ; and yet, the
session of Congress, and the sessions of the
State Legislatures, induce a certain number of
families to lead this life of ease, which relieves
the wife of all care, and offers occasions for
amusement and pleasure.   New Orleans, from
its climate and charming society ; Washington,
as the place of reunion of politicians during the
session, always attract many visitors.   As to life
in summer, it is an universal emigration, rendered necessary by the intensity of the heat ;
and caused, moreover, by the desire for excitement, which every American constantly feels.

The domestic habits of the women of the
South are generally good ; but slavery, increasing the servants of both sexes, sometimes exer-
cises a bad influence on the men, which education is not always sufficient to control.   It is a
bad school for the white children, who live in

contact with degraded servants. This association cannot but be prejudicial.

XVI.

Emigration into the Interior. — Dispersion of Families.

One important fact acts upon the families of the North like those of the South; and it will affect for a long time to come certain parts of the Union, as it is intimately associated with the development of the yet unexplored countries of the vast American continent. Most of the States, especially those which compose New England, send to the West, each year, emigrants taken from their own midst. These are generally young men endowed with great activity, who, not finding in the State which gave them birth the means of comfortable living, and urged on, moreover, by ambition, quit the home hearth, and go to try their fortune at a distance.

When this emigration appears to increase excessively, the local organs of public opinion bestir themselves to make known the grievances of the community, and endeavor to check the depopulation, — which affects all, but especially the laboring classes. A religious journal,* in New York, only lately showed the general consequences of this interesting fact, stating that it greatly affected the family, religion, the sacred calling, agriculture, etc., — in fine, all which forms the foundation of the social edifice.

I shall here confine myself to specifying the object of these complaints, by saying that the immediate consequences of this emigration are the scattering of the members of the same family, and the consequent loss of *bons traditions ;* the withdrawal of the most vigorous and energetic portion of the population, which in course of time must involve the degeneracy of the race ; the great disproportion of the sexes which occurs locally, and, consequently, an excess of unmarried women ; and the necessity of calling for European emigration, to fill up the void, and give labor the arms which it needs. But this auxiliary itself is not without inconvenience ; for its action may some day distort the primitive character of the people. Such are, briefly, the principal results of emigration to the interior ; results which, according to circumstances, may act as most powerful dissolvents.

* The New York Weekly Examiner, Jan. 22, 1857.

XVII.

Education of the American Family.

"What, then, is needed," demanded Napoleon of Mme. Campan, "for the proper education of the youths of France?"—"Mothers," she replied.

Where shall we find them in the United States, if this deplorably restless life continues? It is not enough that a mother attends to the physical development of her children, — that is but the protection of maternity. She must do more ; she must, above all, watch over their instruction, and, as far as possible, herself take part in their education, — a distinct pathway in the work of life. Education will consist in opening the hearts of her children to generous sentiment and elevated thoughts, teaching them to practise religion, and, above all, to comprehend the spirit which vivifies its practice. She is to inculcate the sense of duty, resignation, sacrifice ; in a word, all which strongly fortifies man, by forcing him to reflect, and rely upon himself, in order to struggle successfully with the trials of life.

If you ask instructors, they will reply that the

father of the family takes little part in the education of his children, — he has not the leisure.
As to the mother, her will is easily overcome
by theirs, — either because she brings but a
distracted attention to the discharge of her
duty, or that the independence which her children so readily acquire opposes an invincible
obstacle. Teachers thereby lose their true *point
d'appui:* their authority is but a phantom ; for,
so soon as discipline is maintained, or severity
exercised, they at once lose their pupil.

I do not mean here to speak of University
instruction, which belongs in another order of
ideas, and applies only to a limited number of
young men, in comparison with the mass.

As respects primary and secondary education, the average age at which the pupils quit
their studies, is from twelve to fourteen years.
What can they know at that age ; and what
becomes of them on leaving school ? They go
into a lawyer's or merchant's office, or into business. They soon receive a salary of four or six
hundred dollars, and from this time become
independent of parental control. It is one of
the traits of new manners. What will society
gain by this ? Fortunately, there are a goodly
number of families whom one portion of these
irregularities has not as yet affected, and who

will not recognize themselves in the sketch which I have above made. But the evil is on the increase ; and, as the ideas of business, money, and haste predominate, the danger is serious.

The education of young girls appears to be more carefully attended to, either because mothers feel more competent to watch over it, or that the lady teachers, in charge of their studies, know how to render these more attractive. And on this point it may be permitted me to pay a just tribute of eulogium to the French ladies who have established schools in the United States. Their methods of teaching seem to me superior to those of the Americans, and they have, moreover, the art of giving a tone of good breeding to the young girls intrusted to their care which makes itself appreciated. The ladies of New York, Philadelphia, Baltimore, New Orleans, and other cities, who have been educated in this school, or animated by it, have something in their manners which reveals the source from which they are derived.

Ideas in America do not yet seem to be sufficiently settled in reference to the range of women's education. This is often superficial ; at other times it embraces the Latin language, mathematics, trigonometry, algebra, etc. I have sometimes asked the Principals of schools why the exact sciences were brought into this range of studies, and the reply has generally been, that it was rather with the intention of balancing the natural frivolity of the girl than with the idea of increasing the amount of her knowledge. I can hardly believe in the success of this correction, however useful it may be to make a trial of it. That which is only transient, particularly in dry matters, leaves no durable impression ; and we run the risk of spoiling what is natural, in attempting to mould it.

XVIII.

Reforms in the Condition of the American Woman.

Although the education of women is generally kept within its proper limits, yet there are female reformers whose ambitious aspirations would extend its field indefinitely. We have seen above, that there are some women in the United States who are tormented with the desire of reform in all that respects their sex, and who wish to exercise the same civil, and even the same political, rights as the men of their country. They wish to be American citizens, with the privilege of voting at elections, becoming members of the Legislature, appointed to public offices, and I know not what, — perhaps, become President of the Union! Others, less ambitious, only demand access to the public lectures of the schools of law, of medicine, and of theology, with the right of taking diplomas and practising as advocates, physicians, and ministers of religion.

We may rest assured, that the majority of these demands, which are exorbitant, will meet with an invincible resistance each and every time they are put forth. When more modest, and more in unison with our social condition, the claims of women no doubt will not fail to meet with the reception due to them in the Legislatures ; as, in the opinion of enlightened men, no reason exists for refusing woman now-a-days such civil rights as she enjoys in France.

We see the advance which reform has already made outside of the restricted circle of which I have spoken. These are so many truths which creep into society, awaiting but the majority, to make them held sacred as principles.

XIX.

The Female Physician.

In the professional path, women have not met
with an equal success in contending with public
opinion, or with, what they call, prejudice.   Up
to the present time, at least, they have not succeeded in forcing their way into the schools of
law, and being admitted to the bar, in spite
of the efforts they have put forth on various
sides to accomplish this important result.   But
failure to-day does not insure it to-morrow ; and
it may be that in one of the three and thirty
States, especially the new ones, there may be
found a place where some men, fond of change,
will wish to try this.   And who knows if the
New World is not destined to produce, I will
not say a Demosthenes, but a female Cicero ?

As respects medicine, the attempts have been
more fortunate, although here there has been but
partial success, — yet quite encouraging.   Thus
there has been formed in Boston a special medical school for women, and another in Philadelphia.   The one at Boston has received support
from the Legislature and the citizens.   The one
at Philadelphia is only sustained by subscrip

tions from the admirers of this novelty. Besides this, the medical schools of Syracuse, N. Y., and of Cincinnati, Ohio, admit female students to the regular lectures of these institutions. I would add that a certain number of women have taken their diplomas, and practise medicine in many parts of the Union.

These results, limited as they are, give good omen for the future, if the women who undertake this career only commence with a solid instruction as a foundation, and do not hasten to begin practice before having acquired in the hospitals the experience which alone can command for them a legitimate and lasting success.

Moreover, medicine is the only — at the same time, scientific and practical — branch, where unprejudiced minds can admit the co-operation of females. There are many circumstances where the physical sufferings of women would claim, as their first confidants, persons of their own sex. There are ills which the female from modesty reluctantly confides to a physician. She suffers a long time before doing this ; and sometimes, when she has become resigned, it is too late. If, on the contrary, she could at once address a woman of professional experience, she might have found a relief for the evils which care in season would have remedied.

These reasons are not, however, sufficiently conclusive for the mind of the majority; and the best way is to await the experiment commenced, for proofs of the success of the trial.

It seems in place here, as several years have elapsed since the establishment of these schools, to quote some extracts from a letter to the "Boston Medical and Surgical Journal," Sept. 27, 1866, by Professor H. R. Storer, who says: "On the one hand, I have desired to do what I personally could towards the real enfranchisement of women; and, on the other, I have thought that, by elevating the few women who might be better educated than the mass of those of their sex assuming medical honors and responsibilities and masculine appellations, our profession might be purged, to a certain extent at least, of many claimants utterly unfitted for its membership. . . . It is sufficient for me to say, that, despite certain exceptional cases upon which so much stress has been laid, exceptions in every sense of the word, I think that the experiment has been a failure; and that, were there no other reason than for a physiological one, perfectly patent, though its importance has been so much lost sight of, women can never, as a class, become so competent, safe, and reliable practitioners, no matter what their zeal or opportunities for pupilage." After speaking in commendation of one or two female medical practitioners, Dr. Storer says: "Such are, however, at best, but very exceptional cases; and I am driven back to my old belief, — the same that is entertained by the mass of mankind, — that, in claiming this especial work of medicine, women have mistaken their calling; a belief that, contrary to assumptions that have been made by certain interested parties, I have found to be generally held by ladies of true refinement and delicacy, and by the majority of female patients, no matter what their station in life." — *Note by Translator.*

XX.

Women as Ministers of Religion.

If there are women who believe themselves called upon in professional life to relieve physical evils, how much greater is the number of those who consider themselves as still better endowed to afford the mind soothing consolation, so necessary in this harassing and vexatious life, where man is — if I may so express myself — beside himself, and without a moment for holy meditation.

Without denying any of the gifts which God has liberally distributed to woman, may we not say that the consolations of the spirit are of various natures, and that the field reserved for her in this is limited. All within the domain of religion claims a freedom from wordly passions, without which the soul cannot be elevated ; and our organization is not so immaterial that the choice of a mediator between God and ourselves can be a matter of indifference.

May we not fear that in this forlorn state, when the soul has no secrets, and confidences are expressed with tears, — man may be misled, having only as guide a female preceptor ; and the creature sometimes, perhaps, rather forget the Creator?

I do not know whether the American female reformers have thought over these problems, and others which I refrain from following out. I do not know what solution they would give them; but, according to all appearance, that which would cause me to doubt has ceased to be an objection for them, since their ambition has carried them so far as to desire to minister religion. It seems, their attempts in this direction have not been without some success. And a remarkable fact is, that they have not gained access to one of the new sects which spring up so easily in the United States, but into a denomination already quite old, renowned for its austerity, and its attachment to old traditions, — I mean the Presbyterians. This, at least, is what occurred in the House of Representatives during the session of 1856–1857.[*]

Each year the House, at the commencement of its session, chooses by ballot the chaplain who performs the religious service. In one of the preparatory sittings of which I speak, the names of various ministers were proposed to the assembly; and amongst the number figured that

* Richmond Whig, Jan. 7, 1857.

of Miss Antoinette L. Brown, a ministress of
the Presbyterian denomination. At the reading
of this name, a member arose and made a motion of order, asking if there was any precedent
for nominating a woman for chaplain.

The chairman replied that it was for the House
to decide. Another member formally opposed
the nomination of a female candidate, saying,
" that Saint Paul had ordained that women
should preserve silence in the church, and thus
it would be a neglect of this great apostle's
maxims to choose one for chaplain."

This spirited *à-propos* cut short all debate.
The vote was proceeded with without discussion,
and the feminine candidate rejected on principle.

It is a fact that women have been invested
with sacred office in the Presbyterian denomination, which presupposes theological studies, if
not at the seminary, at least with ministers
of this sect.* According to all appearances,
these occurrences are rather rare. But who can
say when they will cease in a country where it
is so loudly asserted, that all the problems of life
have been wrongly studied, and that they must
be solved again. It is needless to say that
Catholicism opposes these sort of novelties with

* See Appendix, No. 1.

an energy which results from its fundamental principles.

XXI.

The desirable Role for the American Woman.

But, if there are fields where the ambition of some women mislead them, there is a much more natural object which they should seek to attain ; for it seems indicated as connected with their mission in society. In America, more than anywhere else perhaps, women should be the centre of the reunion of men engaged in public affairs.

What is in reality the case now-a-days ? Public life is confined within the narrow circle of purely local interests. Foreign politics belong only to Congress, and it is but rarely concerned with them. The question of slavery alone offers some variety of opinions which may give activity to the mind, but has been argued for so many years, that, whatever efforts are made to rejuvenate it, it but repeats itself. The only thing that is new is that a few more ambitious persons desire to make it a stepping-stone to arrive at power. Such a life has nothing to enlarge the mind, although it is frequently combined with quite individual ideas, often opposed to the general welfare. The peculiarity of this condition is, that it draws the man within a more or less limited circle of interests, and buries his natural qualities.

A distinguished man, the Reverend Henry Ward Beecher, has said with much truth, that what is lacking in the American is mirthfulness, — that is to say, capacity for enjoyment, that relaxation of mind unattainable by men who are devoted to business; in a word, true happiness, where interest is but false coin.

Is not the sphere of woman most naturally indicated, in a society thus constituted? We cannot reproach her with incapacity, as she does not lack intelligence and vivacity of mind. Her presence at the reunions of men could not but refine manners, which too much recall the rudeness and uncouth manners of another age. She would, moreover, introduce an agreeable diversity in the subjects of conversation, which are at present fatally stereotyped, and which give the national mind a tint so uniform as to be almost monotonous. Women themselves would profit by these relations; their minds would gain in solidity an equivalent for the refinement and delicacy which they imparted to the men.

But, to attain this result, the reform must be commenced in the bosom of the family. The husband must consent to associate his wife with all his interests, with all his intimate thoughts, and make her truly his confidante. This would be an indispensable preparation, and the family would be the first to receive the benefits. Here is the desirable role for women; it is vastly above those chimeras which some weak minds cherish, and which will but prove an illusion for themselves and society.

M. de Tocqueville, whose testimony the Americans will not refuse, wrote Mme. Swetchine his ideas of woman's role in society, and he says, (Letter of Oct. 20, 1856):*

"Nothing has more struck me, in my already somewhat long experience of public affairs, than the influence which women always exert in these matters; an influence greater, the more indirect it is. I do not doubt that they give to every nation a certain moral tone, which finally manifests itself in politics. I might mention by name a large number of examples which would illustrate what I say. A hundred times, in the course of my life, have I seen weak men show true public virtue, because a wife was at their side who sustained them in this path, not by advising this or that particular act, but by exercising a strengthening influence upon the manner in which they should in general regard duty, or even ambition."

* Mme. de Swetchine, by M. de Falloux.

M. de Tocqueville, in rendering all homage to this salutary influence of woman, does not conceal that of an entirely opposite character which she may exercise upon her husband, from a sordid or personal interest. But the more women are kept aloof from the current of social life, the less will they be able to face danger and strengthen themselves to meet it, and thus encourage the companion of their life. This is one of the principal purposes of woman's education, in a republic worthy of the name. And, if the Americans have neglected it till now, it is perhaps but in remembrance of woman's position in England, although in reality no similarity exists between the institutions of the two countries.

XXII.

Prohibition of Marriage with Colored People.

So far, I have considered marriage only as respects the white race. Let us see what the Americans have done in this matter for the colored race.

Notwithstanding the great liberty allowed in contracting marriage, there is yet a very charac-

teristic prohibition which should be here mentioned, as it is a trait in morals which proves
how far the antagonism of the white to the other
races has gone in America, even in those parts
of the Union where slavery is prohibited. In
several States, we might say in the majority,*
the local statute prohibits marriage of whites
with the Indians, negroes, and mulattoes, whatever the degree of whiteness of the skin of these
latter. But where the statute is silent, or even
favorable to this sort of alliance, the force of
prejudice is such that no one would dare to
brave it. It is not the legal penalty which is
feared, but a condemnation a thousand times
more terrible. If such a marriage should take
place, especially between a white woman and a
colored man, scandal would be at its height.
It would be such a disgrace to the woman that
she could never free herself from it, and for
safety would have to leave the district where the
union had occurred. It cannot be denied that
such marriages sometimes happen, but it is
always amongst the lowest classes of the community; and, even there, it is not always safe
for the persons braving established ideas, since
among the lower the prejudice of race is as

* Bishop, On Marriage and Divorce, § 223.

deep rooted as in the upper classes, perhaps even more so. But, somewhat curiously, it has been found that within the last few years, in two of the free States, more women than men of the white race have married colored people.

However, these cases are so few that they are not of appreciable importance.

XXIII.

Marriage of Slaves between themselves prohibited by Law.

Shall I speak of the marriage of slaves? Held both as a chattel, and as a being responsible before God and the law, it would seem as if this thinking *thing* ought to be authorized to contract a legitimate union, in order to better associate his life with the idea of duty and the family,—two great elements of civilization. Yet it is quite otherwise. No colored man, while a slave, has the right of legal marriage with another slave or with a free person. He is condemned to a promiscuous intercourse, which may often have the appearance of marriage, but which as often varies and fluctuates at the will of his brute nature, and is not conducive of any civil benefit. The master has always the right to break the natural relation, slight as it may be, which the slave has formed, even by his consent. And, as the law refuses to regulate this tie, there is no recognized paternity. Man and wife may be separated, father and mothei from their children, at the master's will! It is degradation inflicted upon misfortune! It is overthrowing the most elementary ideas of morality! It is a violation of the precepts of the church! See what Pope Adrian I. has said on this subject:

"According to the word of the Apostle, and also of Jesus Christ, no one should discard the sacraments of the church, neither free man or slave ; so likewise in no wise is it permitted to prevent marriage between slaves. Although these marriages may have been contracted in spite of the refusal, and against the wish, of the masters, yet they should in no wise be dissolved." *

St. Thomas was still more explicit. He openly declared, "that, in relation to marriage, slaves ought not to be subject to their masters." †

To defend the system of legislation of the Southern States, it must be proved that there

* De Conjug. Serv., lib. IV. t. ix. cap. i.

† See Balmès, Le Protestantisme comparé avec le Catholicisme, t. i. p. 146 (Bruxelles, 1854), 2e q. 104, art. 5.

are two Bibles and two Gospels, — one for the whites, and another for the blacks. If not, then they must cease to say, that they wish to elevate the moral condition of the slave, to render him amenable to civilization. His welfare is never consulted in these sort of illegal unions ; which are allowed or prohibited according to the personal interest of the master. They are tolerated, even encouraged in the United States ; because, the slave trade being prohibited, and the laborers needed, great attention is paid to the multiplication of the black race. On the other hand, in Cuba, where the trade introduces surreptitiously a large number of new slaves each year, at moderate prices, the promiscuous intercourse between the servants of the black race is prevented as much as possible ; because the care of their progeny would be onerous to the master.

Such is the varying and mobile morality of slave countries ! And, as if it was not enough the business of the slave to increase the stock of this kind, the whites do not hesitate to lend their aid. In this, we do not blush for morality, but for marriage. Sadly confused ideas of morality among a people who profess to be religious, and where the sins of the white are traced in the traits and color of the mulatto !

XXIV.

Counterfeit of Marriage with Mulattresses.

What shall I say of the lot of the young, free mulatto girls, whose color by successive crossings has become white, or nearly so ? In the South, the law, which in this only reflects the morals, absolutely refuses them legal union with the whites ; and, on the other hand, the superiority of their education, as well as the luxury in which they are brought up, places them much above a marriage with a man of color. Hence a false and cruel position, which weighs upon their whole existence.

These women are often pretty : some are really beautiful. They have a graceful and easy carriage, and not a drop of dark blood that has found its way into their veins but gives a charm to their persons. By an education equal to that of young white girls, it is early sought to develop their natural qualities. Some are sent to Paris to complete their education, and nothing is spared to render them worthy of a better lot than that which awaits them. Great effort is made to marry them in Europe ; for what should not be tried to aid their escaping the dreadful alternative of perpetual celibacy, or prostitution, so fatally pointed out. It is under this latter class that the majority of those who live in New Orleans come, — a city where, being more numerous than elsewhere, they form a separate caste. Here this irregularity of life takes a form quite peculiar, which is, as it were, an aspiration towards a better existence, and a sort of a *mise en demeure* made to society to open its ranks for those worthy to enter them.

The whites are easily captivated by the natural attractions of these women, especially if they are heightened by education and powers of pleasing. But, as a legitimate union is impossible, a negotiation is entered into for a *quasi* marriage, and the affair proceeds as if there was a legal bond. The suitor, who has offered himself and been accepted by the young girl, is generally sent to the mother, who conducts the business portion of the affair. She informs herself most thoroughly with regard to his character, habits, and the resources at his command ; and, if all confirms the first impression in respect to him, a contract is made. The white man binds himself to establish the young girl in a style of life and comfort similar to that which she has enjoyed till then, sometimes even superior in certain respects ; and, in anticipation of its happening that he may one day desert her, he engages to pay a fixed sum, to insure her, and the children she may have by this union, a comfortable position.

These agreements being made, a house is rented in a special quarter of the city, where the young couple establish themselves. The woman maintains her former relation with connections and friends ; and the man, who is attached to her, finds himself more or less engaged in these family ties, which are for him a sad reverse to that condition which presented itself so seductively. It is said of these women that they are susceptible of deep attachments, and a fidelity above suspicion. They give a charm to the household, are often orderly and economical, and some of them shame the prejudice which proscribes them. Worldly fear obliges the man to throw a more or less impenetrable veil over this portion of his life, in order to be still admitted into society. He cannot abandon relations and friends without desiring to return ; and finally the time comes, when, waking from a long dream, sometimes at the importunity of creditors, he meditates contracting a legitimate marriage, in order to establish a real family, and make good the loss which such errors too often create. But he cannot do this without first breaking his former engagement. Right and duty trace for him the path to follow.

But sometimes, a return to the past, disagreeable comparisons, a thousand circumstances, will make him regret, too late, having abandoned the first object of his choice. He hesitates, then falls back into these relations again, and becomes criminal perforce of weakness.

But, if faithful to his legitimate wife, and breaking off forever his first engagement, he acts honorably towards the colored woman by paying her the promised sum. These partings sometime cause deep pain to the deserted women, and render them all the more worthy of interest. But, if the separation takes place without regret, they are in the condition of widows, who only await a favorable opportunity to contract a new engagement; and all conspires to offer what they desire.

These unions give birth to children, brought up under the ban of the law and society, which are their natural enemies, — an inseparable consequence of every violation of established order.

A high dignitary of the Catholic Church told me, that the clergy, pained at seeing the majority of young colored girls falling into these immoralities, and noticing that they did not yield

till after the first taking the communion, to
which they attach great value, adopted this
rule : that none of them hereafter should be
admitted to participation in this sacrament, unless they and their mothers obliged themselves,
by a sort of oath, to live honestly by their labor,
and refuse every illegitimate union.

For some time no infraction of the rule was
noticed ; but, insensibly, laxity crept in, seduc-
tions assailed these young girls : a future without
end was always before them ; the contagion of
example, the desire of being well off, — all combined to cause these poor victims to yield, and
this form of promise had to be abandoned, that
it might not be too long a witness of its own
inefficiency, and in order not to expose those
who made it, while yet so young, to scandalously
violating it with impunity.   So that, at present,
in spite of the fatherly remonstrances addressed
to these young girls before the communion, in
spite of every measure which solicitude for the
future could suggest to the clergy, it is very difficult for them to resist any length of time this
current of depravity.   Yet there are honorable
exceptions, all the more meritorious as they must
ever contend against an implacable prejudice
and an incessant allurement.   May we not hope
that a day will come, when a legitimate marriage

will be the recompense of such efforts made to
deserve it. This is doubtful, if the prejudice
of race remains as strong as it is now seen to
be. Moreover, the illegitimate birth of these
colored girls is an obstacle of another nature,
which seems to be a justification for the severity
of opinion. Nevertheless, would it not be better
to legalize by marriage an existing irregular
union, when the woman, faithful to her only
affection, justifies in other respects also the
right which the law shall grant her? These are
questions too important, for the legislator not to
treat them with circumspection, and yet there is
no disinterested person but will admit, that the
actual condition is the very worst that can be.

XXV.

Mormons.

I will not give the name of marriage to the
immorality introduced by the Mormons, and
which is not less revolting to Americans than
to foreigners.* First established at Nauvoo, on
the banks of the Mississippi, they were soon

* See Appendix, No. 2.

driven from this den of corruption, and their
temple burned; as if to show that fire alone
could purify this pestiferous atmosphere. They
sought refuge beyond the Rocky Mountains,
but there, as at Nauvoo, they are branded by
general sentiment; and, without European emigration, especially from England, furnishing
them recruits, they are destined to die out :
for we must render this justice to the Americans, that all which openly violates the sacred-
ness of the family is deeply repulsive to them.

XXVI.

Celibacy Proclaimed as a Principle by the Shakers.

It is worth noticing, how all sorts of eccentricities rendezvous in this land of independence.
At the same time that we see polygamy pushed
to its utmost limits, there exists a sect called
the Shakers whose principal object is the most
absolute celibacy. Their life has none of the
asceticism of the anchorite, or the holy meditation of the cell. They live in a sort of a community composed of men, women, and children ;
and all practise the continence which they
preach. Their morals are known to be irre-

proachable. Their fixed idea is, that, according to the Gospel, and particularly according to the second revelation made to their foundress, celibacy is the only means of obtaining regeneration of the spirit. Further on, I will give some particulars in regard to this sect.* At present, I would merely say, it is a matter of surprise that it should have been established in America, where, from tradition, marriage has always been held in great honor, and where it has contributed so much to the prosperity of the country. This is as yet the only sect that has protested against the commandment of the Scriptures, "to increase and multiply;" and it is doubtful if this Protestantism will have the same success as Luther's. Should it be otherwise, we shall no doubt see a modern Metellus † arising to reinvigorate the institution of marriage. But the American is too prudent to admit such innovations. He will never be the one to shut the great book of humanity.

* See Appendix, No. 3.

† It will be remembered, that the censor Metellus, seeing the great diminution of citizens, proposed to the Roman people to require all the celibates to marry. "Romans," said he to them, "if we could live without women, we should be saved great trouble; but, since nature has willed it that we cannot live comfortably with them, and without them we cannot live at all, we should regard the perpetuity of the State rather than our own contentment."

XXVII.

Divorce.

If the law shows itself so indifferent, so improvident, at the commencement, neglecting to surround marriage with precautions and protective formalities, should it be severe, if a time comes that finds the union ill-assorted and the chain too heavy? Two means are presented to meet this situation, — separation and divorce. Considerations of various character affect this subject. Religion, political economy and social advancement all act diversely; as we have example in the past.

There is, perhaps, no point upon which there has been such diversity of opinion, as in respect to the principle of divorce itself, and the causes which should determine it. Certain persons, and Milton was of the number, would not only have divorce possible for both the married persons, but also the right of repudiation, which according to the law of Moses belonged to the husband alone. Milton said, " that marriage was created for man, but that woman was created for marriage." And he asserts, in the same train of ideas, " that full and unreserved importance should be allowed those mental causes, which, though just in themselves, cannot be carried into law, since there is no human balance that can weigh them."* So, in this system, the husband is both judge and plaintiff; he has not only the law, but the jurisdiction, — which decides without appeal.

In Greece and Rome, during the early periods, the right of repudiation was granted the husband, in imitation, more or less exact, of the Jewish law. But morals relaxed in consequence, and divorce was substituted for repudiation; so that the wife, as well as the husband, had the right of appealing to its decision.

Christianity came, and proclaimed a new law, holding that man could not sunder what God had joined together. Marriage became a sacrament; and, at a single stroke, repudiation and divorce were annulled. The struggle to establish these principles was ·long; but, in the twelfth century, opposition finally ceased, and victory was complete. Affairs changed their aspect during the fifteenth century, when the Reformation commenced. Then, both the sacrament and the law of indissolubility were denied. And,

---

* Milton's Prose Works; and Bishop, On Marriage and Divorce, § 288.

although Catholics remained faithful to this law, Protestants chose not only ancient repudiation, but also divorce for both husband and wife.

Milton lived while this law was in force; but his influence, interested as it was, could not effect a change of the law and a renewed acceptance of repudiation. A dissolution of the tie is now considered possible, rendering the wife the equal of her husband; and yet she cannot present the same claims for divorce as he.

To regard the husband only, is to look at but one side of the question, and to forget that social interest should have more weight in this matter. Society has the right, and should frown at disagreements which can have nothing real in them, and which would give way to serious considerations, if they were viewed in the light of calm reflection. Hence the guards with which divorce is surrounded in some countries, to prevent its degenerating into license.

The example of Pagan Rome should have been sufficient to enjoin a stricter sense of duty on the Christian legislator of our day. In reality, men and women could at that date be divorced for the most trivial causes; and the abuse of this power was pushed to the extreme. St. Jerome relates that he assisted at the fu-

neral of a woman who had had twenty-two husbands.   And Seneca says, that in his day a
woman counted her years, not by the names of
the consuls, but by the number of her husbands.
Can we admit such loose morality in our day?
If marriage itself is partly a sacrifice, should it
not be the role of the law to regulate it, by
endeavoring to reconcile the necessities of
society and of the married pair?   To that, all
good legislation should tend.

This recalls what used to occur in Zurich
under similar circumstances.   When the married couple made an application for divorce,
based on incompatibility of temper, the magistrate, according to the customs of the country,
had the couple applying shut up in an isolated
tower on the lake.   They remained there fifteen
days, obliged to inhabit the same room, having
only one bed, one chair, one knife, one fork;
so that they were entirely dependent upon each
other for their mutual comfort.   If, after this
trial, they persisted in their demand, then the
ordinary procedure commenced, and the tribunals decided.   It is said, that quite often this
preparatory trial sufficed to cause abandonment
of the application for divorce, at first warmly
solicited.

Let us now see how the Americans have

profited by the experience of the past, and after
having been prompted to wrong legislation
concerning marriage whether they have done
better in that which relates to the dissolution of
the bond.

XXVIII.

Numerous Causes for Divorce.

The law of divorce is not the same in all the
States of the Union. Each one, besides the
Common Law of England, has a particular statute upon this matter; but there is a general
tendency to adopt the same reasons for deciding
divorce. In America, there is a common name
for two things which in France receive different
appellations. Thus, there is divorce, properly
so called, — which is the dissolution of the tie;
then this is qualified by divorce *a mensa et toro*,
— what we call *separation de corps*. The latter is
only admitted in very few of the States, and
meets with no favor. This separation is considered immoral; since, according to Lord Howell's
expression, it leaves a wife without a husband,
and a husband without a wife. It is celibacy
in marriage. It offers great temptations for

adultery, and punishes the innocent more than the guilty.

I shall only speak here of divorce, properly so called, and not enter into detail in reference to the causes admitted in each State, but merely select a variety of those sanctioned in different sections. This is pretty nearly the list:

1. Bigamy.
2. Adultery.
3. Voluntary desertion for one, two, three, or five years.
4. Absence continued for five years.
5. Imbecility, or mental alienation.
6. Union with a negro, mulatto, or an Indian.
7. A state of vagrancy.
8. Cruelty or abuse of one party by the other.
9. Slighting conjugal duties.
10. Habitual drunkenness during a certain time, and the excessive use of opium.
11. Imprisonment for crimes determined by the local statute.
12. Impotence of either party.
13. Not providing the wife sufficient means of subsistence.
14. The wife's refusal to follow the husband to where he removes his home.

15. Immorality of either party.

16. Either one belonging to the sect of Shakers, — which I spoke of above, and explained their system.

17. One State, Kentucky, has gone so far as to make a law, that, "when a husband announces in the papers his intention of not paying the debts of his wife, she has sufficient cause for a divorce."

There is only wanting in this list the divorce by computation, which Cicero invoked to repudiate Terentia, — not that he had any complaint against her, but that he needed a new dowry to pay his creditors.

XXIX.

Decision left to Tribunals. — Divorces decreed by the Legislature.

Besides the causes for divorce that I have indicated, there exists in some of the States a statutory provision, which is very important, and ought to be adopted in turn by the others. It was said that the courts of justice, according to their discretionary power, could grant a divorce in all cases where they found the demand just and well founded. It cannot be

disguised that such provisions are extravagant
in common law, as they leave the parties to the
mercy, intelligence, integrity and passions of
the judge ; indeed to everything which might
influence his judgment.

But this is not all. In some of the States, the
Legislature decides upon divorce in concurrence with the courts of justice, which is an
additional abuse ; for then these Legislatures
hold in the same hand legislative and judicial
power. We know how accessible they are to
party influences or coteries, and are sometimes
even affected by considerations of the lowest
kind. A proof of this is, that, where this *concur-
rent jurisdiction* exists, it is without hesitation
the Legislature that is appealed to, although the
causes of the divorces declared by them are
much less important than of those decided by
the courts of justice. One can understand this
anomalous omnipotence in England, where Parliament can, without offending the Constitution,
absorb all the power ; which has given rise to
the remark that Parliament has full power to do
what it sees fit to, with but one exception,
namely, that it cannot turn a man into a woman,
or a woman into a man. But, in the United
States, a democratic country, where there is a
fundamental separation of public powers, this

concentration of legislative and judicial authority in the same hand is an anomaly and a
danger.

XXX.

English and American Laws of Divorce compared.

A law so radical could not have been called
forth, except by what was seen in England anterior to the amended Bill of Divorce cited above.
The immoralities arising from the impossibility
of having recourse to the tribunals would make
the American law seem a step in advance. Yet,
if the English law was in fact only applicable
to a small number, on the other hand, it is fair
to state that it recognized but one cause for
divorce, — adultery. This is far from the almost
indefinite power granted to the caprices of the
married couple in America, which tends to nothing less than indirectly producing polygamy.

The new English law has made the courts
accessible to a much larger number ; and, wiser
than the American, it has introduced no innovation in regard to the causes of divorce. It
admits but one as before, namely, adultery. A
longer experience will show the Americans that

they must greatly modify legislation upon this point. The door is too open to license. And it must never be forgotten, that, the older a society grows, the more important it is to watch over its progress, and by applying the curb prevent its hastening its own decadence.

XXXI.

Prohibition of Divorce. — Concubinage legalized in South Carolina.

There is one of the States of the Union, and one only, which stands in contrast to the others in this matter ; for it admits no divorce, legislative or judicial, for any motive whatsoever. This is South Carolina. Does that mean that marriages are better assorted there than elsewhere? " No," replies an American writer, " divorce is just as necessary there as elsewhere in the Union." * But, has the law acted more wisely in making this prohibition, under the same circumstances? It will not be so regarded if we examine this subject more closely : for, in this State, not only is adultery not subject to judicial prosecution, but cannot be a cause for

---

* Bishop, On Marriage and Divorce, § 285.

divorce; and, still further, it receives a sort of sanction from the legislator, by his thinking it necessary to determine by a special statute what portion of his property a married man may give to his concubine, even under pretext of a compact previous to adultery.

It was no doubt thought that with such a tolerance of loose morality, which is no less than legalized polygamy, there was no necessity for the existence of divorce! But the wife cannot avail herself of this law (a tacit homage to the delicacy of her nature), and, besides, immorality is not the only cause for divorce.

However that may be, this law has found its apologists, even in the courts of justice,* as a *contre coup* to the excessive abuse of divorce.

It does not seem to me to require a great effort of reason to perceive, that both systems are equally deplorable, and that the faults of one do not excuse those of the other. In both cases, the woman is more or less sacrificed; and, whatever the alternative, have we the right to be very severe with the Mormons?

* Bishop, On Marriage and Divorce, § 289.

XXXII.

Divorces numerous.

In the United States, we see in everything deeds and acts the most opposite meeting each other, — so true is it that the human mind is far from having found its path, and must yet run a long while into extremes before recovering it.

In opposition to this law of South Carolina, we see in a neighboring State, Alabama, upwards of a hundred divorces annually declared by the Legislature, without counting those granted by the courts.* A little further off, in Ohio, a judge made this remark, "that there was no law more abused in that State than that of divorce; and that a majority of the inhabitants thought, of all contracts, marriage was the least obligatory, and nothing further was necessary to dissolve it than to make an appeal to the competent tribunals." †

This doctrine is nearly that in practice in Indiana, where the law sympathizes strongly with conjugal misfortunes. Hence, the courts of justice are literally crowded with applications

---

* Baltimore Sun, Feb. 22, 1856.
† Bishop, On Marriage and Divorce, § 290.

for divorce, — whose authors, it is true, are very
often citizens of other States.   But their great
number sufficiently proves the existence of facilities there, rarely found elsewhere.   These impro-
vised decisions are not impeded by any question
of legality ; a simple affirmation is sufficient to
prove a residence in the State, and no one
would hesitate to lie to the court in a question
considered of so little importance.

The Washington "National Intelligencer,"
one of the most respectable papers in the Union,
relates,* that Judge Test, in one of the Indiana
courts, in giving his opinion upon a case of
divorce brought before him, said, "that the
advocates of 'free love' (a new sect which finds
love lacking liberty in the United States) could
not ask a statute more favorable to their views
than the law of divorce in Indiana, and that the
polygamy of the Mormons was preferable ; for
it at least obliged husbands to provide for the
subsistence and protection of their wives."   In
reference to this state of things, an anecdote is
told, piquant enough to be mentioned here.   It
seems that a resident of Syracuse (State of
New York) had been deserted for some time by
his wife, who, at best conjecture, had gone to

* Nov. 1, 1858.

the West to obtain a divorce. The husband
had no objection to his wife's demand ; and his
only desire was to know positively, that she had
succeeded, and that he had henceforth full liberty to engage in a second marriage. To avoid
uncertainty, he thought it best to write to the
several District Recorders, and request them to
inform him, if they knew of a divorce concerning
him, that might have been declared in their
jurisdictions. Amongst the replies which were
made him was the following :

INDIANA, Sept. 18, 1858.

DEAR SIR, — There has not yet been an application for
divorce made to our court, in the name of ———— ; but I
think we have divorced half of the citizens of your State,
so that, if we continue in the same train, I imagine, in a
few years, we shall exhaust the marriages of New York
and Massachusetts.

Awaiting opportunity to be of service to you,

I am, etc., etc.

Whatever exaggeration there may be in the
form of expression, the letter of the Indiana
registrar will serve none the less to prove, that
the number of applications for divorce is large ;
and that the courts, thanks to an unwise law, are
crowded with business of this nature.

Throughout the States, it is thought that all
which tends to separate the married contributes

to the increase of population, and that facilitating
the dissolution of the tie is of social utility;
because it allows the parties to seek another
union, better assorted, destined to fulfil the ends
of marriage.

Under the influence of these ideas, and the
legislation which they create, we need not be
surprised that the number of divorces is very
considerable in the United States.   I have said,
above, what the state of things was in Alabama.
In the State of Pennsylvania, at Philadelphia,
a quiet city founded by the Quakers, it has been
stated that during the nine years up to 1856
inclusive, the courts have declared eleven hundred and thirty-five divorces, without counting
those granted by the Legislature, — which are
also numerous.*

In Connecticut, an old colony founded by the
Puritans, a distinguished man, President Dwight,
of Yale College, said, as long ago as 1816,
before an assembly of the State officers, " that
in the city of New Haven alone, then quite
a village, there had been more than fifty divorces granted in the five preceding years, and
more than four hundred in the whole State,
during the same time.   That is nearly one for

* See Philadelphia Ledger, April 17, 1857.

every hundred homes."* Since then, they have increased. If we may credit a Southern paper, which, like its *confrères* of this part of the Union, takes up eagerly any charge against Massachusetts, we shall find that in a single session of the County Court sitting at Dedham, Mass., the last term of 1856, or the first of 1857, eleven divorces were declared for this small circuit, seven of which were for adultery.†
Statistics would give similar results for the other States of the Union. It is useless to dwell longer upon this point.

To the honor of the American women it must be said, that the majority of the divorces are granted at their request, and not against them. It is often in consequence of their husbands abandoning them to seek their fortunes in the West, in California, where the thirst for gold alters all that is noble and pure in human nature, and contributes to the overthrow of all institutions, even those which ought to counteract this deleterious influence.

In the United States, the one who gains the case has a perfect right to contract another marriage, whilst the lot of the defeated one varies

---

* Bishop, On Marriage and Divorce, § 275.
† New Orleans Picayune, March 10, 1857.

according as the special State regards the circumstances, with more or less severity.   Some of the States authorize an immediate second marriage ; others refuse this right during the life of the other party.   But the proximity of the various States allows these prohibitions to be easily avoided : a simple change of residence suffices to attain the object.   This diversity of law upon the same point, in neighboring localities, often produces curious consequences.   Thus it has been thought, that a person could build a house, composed of two distinct buildings, upon the border line between adjacent States : each portion would be in a different State ; so that a man, who could not engage in a second marriage on account of the divorce declared against him, might live alone in one portion of the house, whilst he had established his wife in the other part, where the second marriage was legal under the same circumstances, — thus being on one side a bachelor, and on the other married.

XXXIII.

Legitimation by a subsequent marriage prohibited.

Marriage is not always the result of a first impulse ; it is also an act of reparation which ought to be especially encouraged. In fact, how many unions are formed only to legalize the birth of children previously born. It would seem that the purity of the motive ought always to find grace in the eyes of a Christian legislator. Nevertheless, the American law, which on this point is simply a copy of the English, refuses without pity legitimation by subsequent marriage. One can scarcely understand that in a country of extreme liberty, where there is such indulgence for misdemeanors even the most serious, where society commiserates the guilty and the criminal, where every means are sought to restore the individual who has broken the law, — we can scarcely, I say, understand why it is so inexorable upon this point, as to refuse the *entrée* of the family to those children, the irregularity of whose origin their parents desire to have forgotten. Why is it not seen, that this legitimation is one of the greatest attractions of marriage for those who have at first avoided it. Does not the refusal of it lay a perpetual weight of remorse upon the repentant, and cruelly torture the parents, by striking at their dearest affections? Why is it not seen, that this is including in the same proscription unfortunate beings who must always carry the stigma of bastard upon their brow, and who cannot retain the same respect and regard for their parents as if the original stain had been effaced?

Yet this is the English law, which is the Common Law of the United States, and which has been repudiated in but a single State (Ohio), — where the local statute recognizes, as in France, the legitimation of a natural child by the subsequent marriage of the parents. This cruel law was called forth by an excessive Puritanism, which to-day is quite an anachronism.

The Romans, although very partial to marriage, and prescribing penalties for celibacy, nevertheless admitted concubinage ; that is to say, a *quasi* union between persons for whom no other impediment to marriage existed, but which had nothing obligatory in it, since the parties could break it off at will. In this tolerated commerce, the father of the children was known, and the latter could be rendered legitimate by a subsequent marriage. Such was the last state of the law, when brought under the influence of Christianity.

If the English and Americans examine the records of this law, they will find that several emperors devised various methods of legitimating the birth of natural children, the issue of concubinage. Amongst these was the subsequent marriage of the parents. It was under Constantine (three hundred and thirty-five years after Christ) that the first general statute respecting legitimation appeared, designed to place natural children under the control of the father. This part of the law was developed by his successors, and at the time of the Institutes the result could be obtained in two ways, — an oblation to the *curia*, and subsequent marriage.*

In France, we have borrowed this latter method from the Roman law, and applied it to recognized natural children, — whose position is in some sort identical with those who are the issue of concubinage. In doing this, we have paid true homage to civilization. Let us hope that the Americans, who have already so greatly reformed English law, will take another step in advance, by adopting the principles of the Roman law. By doing this, they can claim to have bettered their civil code.

* Cod. liv. V. tit. xxvii.

XXXIV.

Have Democratic Institutions had a marked Effect upon the Family.
— What is Woman's Influence in American Society.

In speaking of America, it is requisite to be acquainted with what M. de Tocqueville has said ; for he has written the most important work on this country that we have. The facts which he has collected, his method of systemizing them, the official manner which he has adopted, all tend to render them a valuable subject of thought for those who are not content with a superficial view of affairs, but desire to know their whole bearing. M. de Tocqueville's book had a successful *début*, and it gained him an extensive reputation as a writer, which his subsequent works have increased. The Americans attach great importance to his book, an abridged translation of which has been made a classic work for the higher studies at West Point (the chief scientific school in the United States). It is a tribute of encomium, the most delicate and best expressed which could be paid his high intellect. The grand scientific and literary bodies of France have, as it were, made this

reputation sacred, by appropriating to themselves this eminent man, who has thrown so
much light upon the art of observation in the
domain of politics, morals, economy, etc.

But the greater the authority of a superior
man, the more must we guard against the sway
which he may exercise; for, if he perchance
attributes to circumstances which are only incomplete or transient a character of perma-
nency and normality, or if in spite of himself
he yields to the allurement of certain ideas, we
run the risk of receiving that as a trait of the
physiognomy of a people, which, more closely
observed, will often prove but an accident, without real importance.

I studied with care what M. de Tocqueville
has said upon marriage and the family, in order
to see if the facts which I had collected could
be reconciled with the theories which he has
developed upon these important subjects.
Agreeing with him on certain points, I do not
in others; and, as disagreement with a man of
such weight is a serious matter, it must needs
be explained at length. The reader ought to
be thoroughly acquainted with the points in controversy to be able to judge fully of the case: I
therefore will bring before him all the elements
of the discussion, reproducing, as literally as I

can, the principal propositions of M. de Tocqueville. I shall be scrupulous to omit none, both from conscientiousness and as a mark of deference for so noble an opponent.

The learned author, after devoting the principal part of his book to an exposition of democratic institutions as they are seen in the United States, and to the development of his theories upon this form of government, finally endeavors to show what is the influence of democracy in America upon morals, properly so called. Woman and the family are among the prominent points of this study. He devotes a few chapters to these, in which the facts apply more or less happily in support of his doctrines.

The author examines, first, the position of the young girl. He finds that,* "among almost all Protestant nations, they are far more the mistresses of their own actions than they are in Catholic countries. This independence is still greater in Protestant countries like England, which have retained or acquired the right of self-government." He thinks, † "that in the

---

* De la Démocratie en Amérique, vol. IV. p. 71, 5e. édition.

The words of the American translation of De Tocqueville are quoted, and sometimes, for the sake of clearness, the quotation is more full than Mr. Carlier's. — *Note by Translator.*

† Idem, p. 72.

United States the doctrines of Protestantism are combined with great political freedom and a most democratic state of society, and nowhere are young women surrendered so early or so completely to their own guidance."

Long before an American girl arrives at the age of marriage, her emancipation from maternal control begins. She has scarcely ceased to be a child, when she already thinks for herself, speaks with freedom, and acts on her own impulse. The great scene of the world is constantly open to her view. Far from seeking concealment, it is every day disclosed to her more completely, and she is taught to survey it with a firm and calm gaze. Thus the vices and dangers of society are early revealed to her. As she sees them clearly, she views them without illusions, and braves them without fear; for she is full of reliance on her own strength, and her reliance seems to be shared by all who are about her." Thus* "she is remarkable rather for purity of manners than for chastity of mind;" "and they hold it of more importance to protect her conduct than to be over-scrupulous of her innocence."—"A democratic education is indispensable, to protect women from the dangers

* Idem, p. 73.

with which democratic institutions and manners surround them."

To more fully illustrate his views, the author compares* "the cautious and reserved education of the young French girl with the freedom of the American; and the preference is, no doubt, in favor of the American system." Such are the principal points indicated by the author.

I have had occasion to notice, in the course of my work, the marked differences which exist between the education of the young French girl and that which the American receives. In the education of the latter, compared with that of English girls, I have only indicated the shades of difference. But M. de Tocqueville thinks he saw more in this,—as he, with preconceived idea, accounts for all, by the independent education of the young American girl. Here commences my disagreement with the author.

For one familiar with English society and the English family, this first proposition of M. de Tocqueville will seem rather doubtful: moreover, he fails to compare, in this respect, the United States with England; for he should remember, that, in the latter country, where

---

* Idem, p. 73.   Idem, p. 75.

the organization of society is purely aristocratic, where the law of marriage is especially
made with this feeling, the young girls are educated with the same independence, the same
liberty, the same acquaintance with the dangers
which society offers, as the young American
girl. With them, acceptance has not, as its
prelude, that timid diffidence which is so charming. The fruit has ripened without the flower
which is its lovely precursor. And if we find a
degree of exaggeration of the system among the
Americans, it is but a variation of it, which does
not affect its principal features. When analogous results are produced under the influence
of institutions so different, what has democracy
to do with such matters? Is it not more natural and more just to say, that these manners are
traditional, and brought by the first colonists
from England to America; that they have been
transmitted from generation to generation, and
grown stronger by being favored by democratic institutions, which are, as it were, their
preserver? The political form of government
is not, therefore, their determining cause; it
simply guides them. This it is very important
to notice.

M. de Tocqueville has said, as I above stated,
that the young American girl must be fortified

against the perils with which the manners and institutions of a democracy surrounded her. I have asked myself, What are these perils? But the author quickly undertakes the refutation of his own proposition by saying : *

"Not, indeed, that the equality of conditions can ever succeed in making men chaste, but it may impart a less dangerous character to their breaches of morality. As no one has, then, either sufficient time or opportunity to assail a virtue armed in self-defence, there will be at the same time a great number of courtesans and a great number of virtuous women."

This should reassure us with regard to the perils with which the author at first startled us. But, as if this was not sufficient to fully allay our fears, he says,† "that the Americans always show by their conduct that they consider women virtuous and refined, and that in their presence every one is guarded in his remarks, to avoid obliging them to hear language which might offend them." This being so, the safeguard, it seems to me, would have been less necessary to protect innocence ; and the young American girl, having nothing to fear from democratic manners, would not need a special democratic education.

* Work quoted, p. 91. † P. 102.

After having praised the morals of the Americans, M. de Tocqueville says,* "It is evident, that on this point the Americans are very superior to their progenitors, the English. A superficial glance at the two nations will establish the fact." He defends his remark by saying, "In England, as in all other countries of Europe, public malice is constantly attacking the frailties of women. Philosophers and statesmen are heard to deplore that morals are not sufficiently strict, and the literary productions of the country constantly lead one to suppose so. In America, all books, novels not excepted, suppose women to be chaste, and no one thinks of relating affairs of gallantry." The author considers, that,† "no doubt, this great regularity of American morals originates partly in the country, in the race of the people, and in their religion; but all these causes, which operate elsewhere, do not suffice to account for it : recourse must be had to some special reason. This reason appears to me to be the principle of equality, and the institutions derived from it." There are scattered through these few lines several assertions which it is necessary to separate, in order the better to refute them individually.

* P. 84.　　　† P. 85, work quoted.

1. Greater morality in America than in England.

2. The influence of race and religion.

3. Especially the influence of equality and of democratic institutions.

M. de Tocqueville says that a superficial glance will prove the first of these propositions. I admit with him that observation is superficial, for he does not go to the bottom of the subject, and sees only the surface. It is from this that he will fail to convince. I will do what the author has not done, namely, elucidate the question.

In England, the morals of the family could not have been so pure as in the United States, because, till 1856, divorce and separation existed only nominally for the majority. In fact, the costs of a case of this kind could not be counted less than ten thousand dollars, without reckoning that an enormous length of time must be wasted in struggling through a labyrinth of procedures, complicated and iniquitous, which repelled even those whose fortune allowed of assailing them. Ill-assorted couples were forced to prolong indefinitely an intolerable existence under the same roof ; or to separate, more or less voluntarily, with all the dangers attached to that equivocal and unhappy condition. Hence immoralities, which the law must bear the principal responsibility of.

Suppose, for an instant, the same laws to exist in the United States, the same immorality would probably occur, — a proof of which is the three thousand divorces that are declared every year. A country where divorce and separation are impossible differs widely from one where they are frequent.

In searching further, M. de Tocqueville would have seen, that there was no ground for his argument, and have spared the English. It is to be regretted that he should have trusted to appearances only, which, as he himself has said, afford but a superficial view.

The learned author does not insist upon causes deduced from race and religion, and in reality they would have afforded here no support. The English may appeal to them as well as the Americans. The same blood flows in the veins of both people, and both profess the same religion.

Nothing therefore remained for the author, but to confine himself to equality of condition and democratic institutions, in attempting to establish the superiority of American morals compared with those of the people of Europe.

He explains,* "that where social position and
condition are identical there is nothing to inter-
fere with choice in marriage, and from this full
liberty there can but result fortunate selections,
and hence good morals."

This argument has for him, it is true, all the
appearance of indisputable fact, but, examined
more closely, its refutation readily appears.   If
the question is only in regard to freedom in the
choice of a husband, it must be admitted that the
English girl has not as much as the American.
But, according to the author, this independence
is but nominal for the English girl, since in an
aristocratic country there are lines of demarca-
tion which are a barrier to freedom of choice, —
and which do not exist in a democratic country.   To a certain extent, I admit the force
of the argument.   Yet in England, as elsewhere,
every one living in a fixed sphere, the selections
which would overstep certain limits are so rare
that they cannot authorize a rule so absolute as
that given by M. de Tocqueville.

But I will go further : France, which he regards as entirely monarchical, has, nevertheless,
very democratic civil institutions, comparable
with those of the United States.   Yet following

* Work already quoted, p. 85.

the reasoning of M. de Tocqueville, who does not admit this similarity, we must grant that the morals of the family are less pure in France than in the United States; because in our aristocratic and monarchical country there is, in fact, no equality of condition any more than democracy in our institutions. It is seen that I give the author's statement fully.

If this be so, how is it that among the thirty-six millions of inhabitants of France there are but each year, taking the highest number, about nineteen hundred *separations de corps*, two hundred of which only are for adultery; whilst in the United States, with a population of thirty millions, there is reckoned at least three thousand divorces per year (about one hundred for each State), a part of which are for adultery? I am not informed of the precise number of divorces of the latter nature, but, if one may judge by the information given from time to time in the newspapers, it will greatly exceed that of the *separations de corps* declared in France for the same cause.

It is seen that I oppose positive facts to hypothetical data, thus annulling the conjectures drawn therefrom.

How, now, can American morality be declared superior to that of the people of Europe. It

must, moreover, not be forgotten that the numerous divorces in America are nearly always followed by subsequent marriage, which in the
eyes of many moralists is considered as polygamy and has been called *successive*, to distinguish
it from that which is *simultaneous*.   The author,
desiring to connect everything with institutions,
does not give to religion the influence due to it.
This it is which acts upon the morals much
more than any special form of government.
But in putting religion in the front rank the
author encountered two obstacles.   Supporting Protestantism, England, whose morals he
accuses of being so bad, came in his way;
or, if just towards Catholicism, he invalidated
what he had said in favor of the Americans.
It is, without doubt, under this embarrassment
that religion is seen in the second range of considerations presented by him in this important
matter.

M. de Tocqueville follows the young American into the married state.   He shows her *
"henceforth sacrificing this freedom that she
enjoyed with such pleasure, to resign herself to
the home that is entitled to the name of cloister, such is to be the austerity of her life!"   He

* Work already cited, p. 77.

represents her as a sort of heroine,* "supporting the reverses of fortune of her husband with tranquillity and indomitable energy." And he does not hesitate to attribute these marvellous results to † "the domestic education she has received, — that is to say, to the freedom without limits which she has enjoyed in her young days, and which enabled her to calculate well beforehand the importance of the act which she consummated in marrying."

Looking back on the picture which I have presented above, one may see that the judgment of the young American girl is far from being so matured as M. de Tocqueville imagines. It has its intermissions, and may perhaps fail here as elsewhere. The marriages *ex abrupto*, the misalliances, the unions decided by aristocratic instincts, and the large number of divorces, render any other proof needless.

As to the cloister life, and the sacrifice of everything by the married woman, I regret to lessen the interest which always attaches to devotion and resignation ; but the page of history should not borrow from fiction, and absolute truth alone should find place here.

It must be admitted, that the doors of the

---

* Work already cited, p. 80. † Work already cited, p. 77.

cloister are but poorly fastened, when wives
escape every day for visits, walks, and the thea-
tre, — in a word, for all that corresponds to
European life.

I remember in this connection, to have listened to a sermon, in a Presbyterian church,
by a learned and eloquent preacher. The
sermon turned upon the employment of their
time by wives and young girls. The sacred
orator spoke with guarded and dignified firm-
ness against the abuse of their leisure time by
the American women, in promenading without
purpose, unless that of displaying their extravagance, and of seeing and being seen. He told
them that there was something better to do, and
called their attention to a charitable institution,
which received a certain number of young girls
who were poor, and had ever need of counsel
and encouragement, that would be so valuable
to them, if it came from women of the world
who had no professional function to discharge
with them. The minister recommended ladies
to visit this institution, and others of similar
character, to console these afflicted ones. It
would be, next to their domestic duties, the best
employment of their time, and the best education for the young girls of society.

It is to be regretted, that M. de Tocqueville

did not hear this touching homily upon the duty of the Christian woman. He would have seen, that we are far away from that cloister which he makes us dread ; and that, on the whole, the English woman lives much more retired in her cottage than the American, in spite of her so-called democratic education.

Here is another statement.* "The Americans," says the learned author, "consider marriage as a contract, often onerous, but which they have entered upon meaning to carry out all its clauses ; because there has been full liberty to bind themselves to nothing."

An eminent judge, in the United States, overthrows this edifying theory by saying,† "that, in the State in which he lives, the citizens consider that of all contracts marriage is the one least binding ; and that nothing more is necessary to dissolve it than a simple petition addressed to the competent tribunal." The number of divorces declared each year, with the long list of causes which induced them, more than prove that this remark of the magistrate is applicable to all the States of the Union. In the face of these facts, which are indisputable, what becomes of the theory of M. de Tocqueville?

* Work already quoted, p. 87.
† Bishop, On Marriage and Divorce, § 290.

The author does not conceal his wish, that the wife should hold an equal position with her husband, and he says, " The social movement which brings together the father and son, the servant and master, elevates the woman, and ought to do it more and more, in making her equal to the man." I have expressed this view above, as M. de Tocqueville has done ; but it seems that the movement which has approached servant and master is very slow in producing a similar equality between husband and wife. It must be admitted, that there is not the same connection between the facts of practical life as between the ideas of the author, especially in positions so dissimilar. We have seen above, how, very recently, in two States, the Legislatures have rejected propositions whose object was to grant to woman rights the most moderate that could be claimed for her. And, with few exceptions, general opinion has persisted in leaving her in the inferior civil position she has so long held. Democratic institutions, we see, are much less favorable to woman than our French ones, called monarchical. If it is insisted that institutions are nothing in all this, we still have the right to say that the Frank race is more advanced in civilization than the Anglo-Saxon, recognizing in woman a mind and an aptitude which cannot be doubted ;. we grant her rights in accordance with her faculties, whilst they are obstinately denied her the other side of the Channel and of the Atlantic.

Yet M. de Tocqueville endeavors to maintain, that the position of woman, such as it is, has its advantages ; and he says,* " In no country has such constant care been taken as in America to trace two clearly distinct lines of action for the two sexes, and to make them keep pace one with the other ; but in two pathways which are always different." He thinks, " if, on the one hand, an American woman cannot escape from the quiet circle of domestic employments, on the other hand she is never forced to go beyond it. Hence it is that the women of America, who often exhibit a masuline strength of understanding and a manly energy, generally preserve great delicacy of personal appearance, and always retain the manners of women, although they sometimes show that they have the hearts and minds of men."

I at once avow that I do not admit the logical consequences which the author draws from his proposition. How does the necessity for the wife to occupy herself with domestic cares, and

* Work already quoted, p. 97.

not being drawn from them for other occupations, give hei such judgment and energy so masculine ? What is the connection between these two ideas ? But, granting the justice of the reasoning, why should it not be recognized in the English woman, whose situation is perfectly identical, possessing the same virtues and the same courage. The author has closely observed society in England and in America, as I myself have done, and he cannot say that the English is inferior to the American woman in those qualities which pertain to the other sex.

If the same results are produced among women of the same origin in countries governed by institutions so different, what has democracy to do with it at all.

The author continues, * " The Americans never have supposed that one consequence of democratic principles is the subversion of marital power, or the confusion of the natural authorities in families." — " It seems to me," he says a little further on, "that the American women attach a sort of pride to the voluntary surrender of their own will, and make it their boast to bend themselves to the yoke, not to shake it off." He finishes these remarks by observing,

---

* Work already cited, p. 99.   Idem, pp. 100, 101.

" In the United States, it is not the practice for a guilty wife to clamor for the rights of woman, while she is trampling on her holiest duties."

In reading these passages, which are literally transcribed, I seem to see the early Spartan matrons brought to life, who affected a stoicism that has so long been held up to us as the beau ideal of life, but which now-a-days seems simply an excess of pride. Very fortunately, the American woman is not thus influenced, and does not mar her happy nature by the assumption of conventional virtues which do not belong to this our age. At the domestic hearth, she has her proper position, but she desires also to have her place in the world ; and, if the instigators of reform seek to make it too great, it is the fault of manners, and not of democratic institutions, which the author still brings in, — we know not why. This movement of reform exists everywhere, — in the atmosphere, among all classes of people   There is nothing in it which can be considered anomalous in America.

Must a woman be adulterous, as M. de Tocqueville seems to say, in order to claim legitimate rights.   And supposing even these demands exaggerated, and the form in which they are made exorbitant, as, for example, the protestation made by Miss Stone in her contract of

marriage,* these eccentricities do not in any
way prove immorality on the part of those who
make this mistake. The breeze is towards
reform, and, if it stirs the imagination, it does
not necessarily affect virtue.

The reform movement in favor of women gains
ground; slowly, it is true, but it will surely obtain
for them a reasonable amelioration of condition.
In practical life, we may already see an emancipation, which has been sufficiently remarked
upon, and aspirations still greater hoped for.

It is precisely the opposite of the life of
retirement and sacrifice that M. de Tocqueville
has shown us.

The author concludes his remarks upon this
important subject by the following : †

"As for myself, I do not hesitate to avow, that, although
the women of the United States are confined within the
narrow circle of domestic life, and their situation is in
some respects one of extreme dependence, I have nowhere
seen women occupying a loftier position."

The author undoubtedly refers to what he has
previously said, when speaking of the uncertainty of American fortunes, where he represents the wives "supporting these revolutions
with calm and unquenchable energy, following

* See above, p. 60.   † Work quoted, p. 104.

their husbands to the Western wilds, to share with them the countless perils and privations which always attend the commencement of these expeditions." — * " I have often met, even on the verge of the wilderness, with young women, who, after having been brought up amid all the comforts of the large towns of New England, had passed, almost without any intermediate stage, from the wealthy abode of their parents to a comfortless hovel in a forest. Fever, solitude, and a tedious life had not broken the springs of their courage. Their features were impaired and faded, but their looks were firm ; they appeared to be at once sad and resolute." The author does not doubt, † " that these young American women had amassed in the education of their early years that inward strength which they displayed under these circumstances." He ends by saying, ‡ " If I were asked, now that I am drawing to the close of this work, in which I have spoken of so many important things done by the Americans, to what the singular prosperity and growing strength of that people ought mainly to be attributed, I should reply, To the superiority of their women."

---

* Idem, pp. 80, 81.   † Idem, p. 81.   ‡ Idem, p. 104.

I imagine that Americans who have read these passages in the original, or find them here for the first time, will be a little surprised to learn that their great prosperity is owing to the superiority of their women.

I certainly shall not be wanting whenever homage is to be paid to the virtues and all good qualities of the women of America. But to give them the special credit of the great success of this country is to grant them, not only an exceptional, but a general, superiority of intellect to their husbands, completely at variance with the observation of facts, and with the nature of the thing itself. It does not agree with what several teachers of the higher schools for girls told me, — namely, that the exact sciences are taught, less to increase their knowledge than to counterbalance the natural unsteadiness of their mind.

I admit, with M. de Tocqueville, that the American women are capable of great sacrifices, and perfect resignation in the face of misfortunes which may come upon their husbands ; and that they possess energy sufficient to aid them in restoring their fortune, not by any absolute labor (for custom prevents that), but in following them in the midst of privations, and exposure to the diseases of desolate countries

where they take refuge.   This is a real and
undoubted merit.   But is it true that the influence of a *democratic* education can alone call
forth such grand qualities.

The author says, that he has often seen examples
of self-denial on the borders of the wilderness.
I think the word *often* is too flattering to agree
with facts.   For I myself have also visited the
West, and at a period when it was much more
widely explored than at the time of M. de
Tocqueville's visit to America, and I may say,
that the examples of devotion that he speaks of
seemed to be very rare exceptions, doubtless not
because this devotion had lessened, but that the
occasions for similar sacrifices are fortunately
less common.

If we must take literally M. de Tocqueville's
proposition in regard to the influence of a democratic and Protestant education in producing so
many and such magnanimous qualities, we can
but commiserate women who are born and forced
to live under different institutions.   Catholicism
especially, which has been thought to have called
forth angelic devotion in millions of cases
amongst women of all conditions, may right-
fully claim — and perhaps, if appeal is made to
M. de Tocqueville better informed, rather than
to M. de Tocqueville a little prejudiced, it will

gain — for its flock an equality of position with
Protestant women.   It will not be too urgently
claimed, and no doubt concession will be given.

But let us pass from these generalities, and
take up the facts.   Did M. de Tocqueville see
only, in America, American devotion in the women whom he met on the borders of the wilderness.   Did he not happen to meet the wives of
European immigrants, whom misfortunes, often
unmerited, had driven from their country to seek
in the new world means of subsistence, and the
hope of a better future.

It is true, the large majority of these emigrants have never known opulence, and in this
respect there is no sacrifice in the sense which
the author attaches to it.   But a certain number
have been in easy circumstances, and a proof of
it is their having already carried more than half
a billion of our money to the United States.
Now, the wives of these emigrants, who have
accompanied them, had themselves to experience how toilsome and hard this life of the
wilderness was.   Have *they* exhibited less courage or less resignation than the Americans?
No one would dare say so.   And yet their lot is
worse than that of the women of the new world.
For they come to a country with which they are
unacquainted.   They often even do not know

the language. And they were forced to bid adieu, perhaps forever, to their fathers, mothers, brothers, friends,— to all in this world which holds our most cherished affections. For them it is a perpetual exile ; which it is not for the Americans who are in their own country, and who retain the hope of finally returning to the place which gave them birth. Shall I add, that something still more painful weighs upon the existence of these new-comers. It is the prejudice of race and of religion which pursues them constantly, and gives them neither peace nor rest till after a long period of acclimation. Is not the devotion of these women still more grand than that of the American. And who now would think of saying that it needed a strong democratic and Protestant education to produce such masculine virtues.

But let us look at another point of comparison, yet more striking, and which comes still nearer home to us.

All the world preserves the remembrance of the great catastrophe of the French at St. Domingo. The colonists were either of noble family or rich *bourgeoisie*, and when the massacre commenced there was but a small number of these unfortunates who could, by rapid flight, amidst a thousand dangers, escape this butchery,

and in fragile vessels reach the hospitable
shores of the United States and of Cuba.
Reduced to the greatest extremity, they were
obliged to work for their living, to undergo the
greatest privations, sometimes forced to accept
subordinate positions, in order to escape death
by starvation and misery. All, or at least the
large majority, were successful, and by labor,
privation, and economy acquired, if not wealth,
at least an honorable competency. In the midst
of these uncommon misfortunes, the women
were distinguished by their moral energy, most
complete self-denial, and oblivion of a past, which,
although it recalled lost pleasures, could not abate
their courage. If M. de Tocqueville could have
seen, as I have, in Pennsylvania, in Carolina, in
Cuba, some of the noble remains of an immense
shipwreck, he could, as I, have learned with an
excusable pride the honorable position which
these immigrants, and especially the women,
occupied in public opinion. This remembrance,
wholly French, it would seem to me, ought to
arrest the pen of the learned author, and prevent his granting the American woman, from
theory, a sort of monopoly of the highest virtues,
due according to him to the democratic education of his model.

As to the decisive influence of American

women upon the prosperity and wealth of the
United States, after all that I have said in this
review I must waive the discussion of a proposition which tends to too greatly ignore the husbands of these exceptional women ; whilst there
is evidence to prove that this success is due to
the indomitable energy of the American, — married or single, — and to his self-dependence,
aided by a multitude of external circumstances,
which have great share in it.

I have finished this too long controversy, and
I would sum it up by saying :

1. The very great independence of the young
American girl is mostly due to the race to which
she belongs, to the religion which she professes,
and to the traditions brought from England.
The education which she has received in the
midst of democracy has but augmented this
disposition, without at all determining it. Witness the young English girls, who enjoy the same
independence, slightly less exaggerated.

2. Altogether, the education of the young
French girl, cautious and strict as it may be
considered, does not cause less well-assorted
matches than in the United States, where divorces multiply.

3. The condition of the married woman in
America, in spite of democratic institutions, is

not different from that of the English ; for the laws of both countries refuse them civil rights which the French woman, in a monarchy, has enjoyed for a long time.

4. The life of the American woman is not based upon a sacrifice : she enjoys the same liberty as the women of Europe, and nowhere perhaps is luxurious living so general as in the new world.

5. If misfortunes assail the American women, undoubtedly they know how to support them with courage, and make very great sacrifices. But numerous examples prove, even in America itself, that the women of Europe, belonging to another race, professing another religion, brought up in monarchical countries, when placed in similar positions of misfortune, have shown, without ostentation, a courage, a resignation, a self-denial, which will yield in nothing, if it is not superior, to the virtues of the Americans.

6. The morals of the family in France are not inferior to those of America. The statistics of the two countries give us even an advantage, which I will not call for.

7. The great prosperity of the Americans has nothing to do with the influence of the women, as I have repeatedly proved in the course of this essay. The credit belongs to the Americans

themselves, who ought in justice to admit, as a very efficacious auxiliary, the concurrence of a multitude of circumstances, fortunate and exceptional, — such, I believe, as no other people ever met.

8. We cannot give homage to democracy for the influence upon morals, upon woman, and upon the family which M. de Tocqueville attributes to it ; because we find elsewhere than in America, under the sway of different institutions, morals as good, women as devoted, and families as well regulated.

9. Finally, if there is to be attributed to democracy in America a direct influence upon marriage, upon woman and the family, as M. de Tocqueville asserts, it must, in view of the facts which have been stated in the course of this essay, be admitted that this influence is but an unlimited development of personal independence, — which everywhere and always constitutes a dissolvent, and is far from being an agent of conservatism.

The great differences which I have brought forward between M. de Tocqueville and myself should create in the mind of the reader a desire to ascertain the causes. But it is not for me to enter upon this path. I will only say, that, if modifications in morals and manners in America

have taken place, they have not gone so far as
to show to-day a physiognomy very different
from that which they had when the author observed them.

In fact, I stated above, that, as early as
1816, — fifteen years before M. de Tocqueville's
travels, — the President of Yale College, one
of the most important universities in the United
States, complained bitterly before an imposing
assembly, of the number of divorces that had
already been noticed in Connecticut, — the most
Puritan State of the Union.   If, in 1816, morals
were of a character to be deservedly censured,
it is difficult to admit that they could escape
the careful scrutiny of an intelligent observer.
And, on the other hand, if he had remarked them,
what becomes of his theory of the influence of
democracy upon the morals of the family?

I must stop here.   I end by expressing my
deep regret at these differences ; but I show the
facts and proofs, and all the latter are of American origin, and therefore undoubted, as the
reader will admit.   I shall find myself once
more in presence of M. de Tocqueville upon the
ground of American institutions themselves,
after I have finished the subject upon which I
am engaged.   Sometimes I shall share his opinions, and I hope that such may be the case as

often as possible.   Sometimes also, I shall
disagree with him, but then, as now, we shall
have the same judge to decide.   I shall not
bring forward such disagreements oftener than
there be necessity for, and only under color of
conscientious duty.   I must not forget, that, if
the discussion claims courtesy, history requires
truth without illusion.

XXXV.

Tendency of Morals Fatally Opposed to the Purpose of Marriage.

I approach here, with some regret, a grave
consideration, which is intimately associated with
the object of marriage, and which shows a
noticeable alteration of the morals of the family
in the United States.   I shall not generalize
more than is becoming, and God forbid that I
should ever make a whole nation accountable
for the faults of a few.   But, when men placed
in situations where they are perfectly acquainted
with facts sound the alarm, it must be that the
evil is already great, and threatening to become
more serious.   The Americans, like the English,
have well understood that the immediate object
of marriage is paternity, and, at the same time

that it is a joy for the domestic hearth, it is also an abundant source of wealth for the country. Faithful to these ideas, the American people have practised fully the precept of Scripture, "Increase and multiply;" so that there is probably no nation in the world where the increase of population has been so rapid as in the United States, even aside from European immigration, which has added to this number in proportions till now unheard of.

With the fortune accruing always to honorable labor and prosperous circumstances is felt the desire of living well, and even of luxury. And, as nothing is done in this country in moderation, expenditure is carried to such a point of exaggeration and folly as to yield in no respect to the luxury of Europe. A certain number of married women, who had remained a long time domestic, have given themselves to this frivolity of the age; and, being obliged to find the means of meeting these expenses, and diminishing the cares of their *ménage*, they have come to *economize* in family. If, in general, the idea of economy is associated intimately with that of forethought, it is quite the reverse here. Improvidence produces regret, and regret which is antagonistic to the family provokes to crime. It is thus that we see mothers, whom a legitimate union has blest, repudiating the gift which God has granted them, and suppressing, without scruple, maternity in its hopes. The secrecy with which they envelop it sufficiently attests that their conscience is not at ease ; but, as they have their husbands as abettors, perhaps they persuade themselves that in dividing the fault they diminish the responsibility,— a sad state of morality, which, if it gains ground, will be of a nature to seriously affect the character of the nation.

It must be in justice said to the honor of the medical corps, that physicians, little as they may be esteemed, refuse all complicity with these criminal practices, and openly denounce them. But there are still a sufficient number of men, physicians or not, who draw large profits from this criminal business. For example, in New York, some twenty physicians—or those calling themselves so — are named, whose whole resource consists in this, and whose specialty is recognized by a particular mark attached to their names. Moreover, they contrive to do indirectly that which the law forbids. Thus, advertisements are published in the newspapers of the Union, saying that one must be careful not to take certain medicines in the situation denoted, which signifies that they are recommended in the special case.

Without at all seeking to justify them, we can imagine parents, who, wishing at any price to save the honor of their daughter, compromised in a moment of error, would silence all scruples, heedless of the means used, to escape the shame which public opinion would inflict upon her. But that such practices should be deliberately brought into marriage, with the consent and under the direction of the husband, for a deplorable object, is a lamentable subject for reflection, not only in a criminal point of view, but because it pollutes the mind and depraves the heart of the woman, exposing her, if not to death (which sometimes happens), at least to an irremediable deterioration of health.

Some men of easy morals have gone so far as to consider the man who denounces this immorality not only as singular, but even impertinent. An explanation must here be made, which may to a certain extent extenuate the fault of some mothers.

The Common Law of England, which is also the Common Law of the United States, establishes in this matter distinctions for determining the commencement of life, and according as the attempt was anterior or subsequent to this period there was or was not offence (*dèlit*).* I

* Wharton, On American Criminal Law, § § 1220 and following.

make use of this latter expression, for the law, even in the most unfavorable case, does not recognize any criminality : it is but a simple offence. Science has, however, long ago disposed of these subtilties, which are only based upon the most superficial observations, as M. Orfila has so well proved in his "Traité de Medecine Légale." *

Experience has taught the same in England, and, from that time, the legislator has been engaged in reforming the law. This has been done by three successive Acts, of which the last, passed in the reign of Queen Victoria, is in conformity with the basis of French law. But, in America, with the exception of three, which have more or less filled up the omissions and defects of the Common Law, the several States have held to the principles laid down by this law, without being influenced by the certainties which science has given to public morality. Yet there is, aside from the law, an intimate consciousness, whose empire is supreme, and which no doubt has often arrested the hand put forth to commit the crime. But when this conscience strays, it must be brought back into the path, and all good and honest hearts ought to

* Traité de Medecine Légale, vol. i. p. 226.

unite their efforts to get free from this morbid
atmosphere, which at present envelops the
family.

Physicians have been the first to point out the
evil, and some of them have taken the initiative
by Resolutions whose object was to ask of the
Legislatures of the States new laws, in harmony
with recent English legislation.

But certain people have arrived at such a
degree of hypocrisy, that the medical journal in
Boston which published an inquiry of this character was absolutely reprimanded by one of its
confrères and by private letters, as if publicity,
which is the soul of this country, was not the
best means of branding these lax customs, by
denouncing them in the name of outraged
morality. We may be satisfied of the extent
of the evil by consulting the " Boston Medical and Surgical Journal," to which I have
alluded, — numbers for 13th December, 1855 ;
7th and 28th May, 1857. One of these articles
gives the Report of a meeting of a medical society of Massachusetts at which, after the exposition of grave facts, it was proposed to petition
the Legislature for energetic repressive measures against this public calamity. Another
journal in Boston, more especially devoted to
religious affairs, the " Boston Traveller," of

June, 1857, in speaking of the action of another medical society upon this subject, strongly condemns these same practices. Finally, the "Chicago Tribune," of June 13, 1857 (an influential paper of the West), denounces them as increasing, and calling for severe measures to repress them.

There is, however, a document coming from another point of the United States, which completes the evidence upon this grave subject. I speak of an opening address delivered by a much esteemed Professor of one of the principal medical schools of the United States.* This discourse, which is the introductory to the session of 1854–55, treats of the subject *in extenso.* I quote the original, omitting a few passages :

" We blush, while we record the fact, that in this country, in our cities and towns, in this city, where literature, science, morality, and Christianity are supposed to have so much influence, where all the domestic and social virtues are reported as being in full and delightful exercise, even here, individuals, male and female, exist, who are continually imbruing their hands and consciences in the blood of unborn infants. . . . So low is the moral sense of the community on this subject, so ignorant are the greater number of individuals, that even mothers, in many

* On Criminal Abortion, by Hugh L. Hodge, M.D.   Philadelphia, 1854.

instances, shrink not from the commission of this crime, but will voluntarily destroy their own progeny, in violation of every natural sentiment, and in opposition to the laws of God and man.   Perhaps there are few individuals in extensive practice as obstetricians who have not had frequent applications made to them by the fathers or mothers of unborn children (respectable and polite in their general appearance) to destroy the fruit of illicit pleasure, under the vain hope of preserving their reputation by this unnatural and guilty sacrifice.

"Married women also, from the fear of labor, from indisposition to have the care, the expense, or the trouble of children, or some other motive equally trifling or degrading, have solicited that the embryo should be destroyed by their medical attendant.   And, when such individuals are informed of the nature of the transaction, there is an expression of real or pretended surprise that any one should deem the act improper; much more, guilty: yea, in spite even of the solemn warning of the physician, they will resort to the debased and murderous charlatan, who for a piece of silver will aid them in the commission of the crime, at the risk of the life of the ignorant or guilty mother.

"This low estimate of the importance of the condition is by no means restricted to the ignorant or to the lower classes of society.   The evil affects educated, refined, and fashionable women; yea, in many instances, women whose moral character is in other respects without reproach. The contagion has reached mothers who are devoted with an ardent and self-denying affection to the children who already constitute their family."

The Professor finishes by saying:

"In view of the influence which medical science must exert on these questions, it seems hardly necessary to repeat, that physicians, medical men, must be regarded as the guardians of the rights of infants. They alone can rectify public opinion; they alone can present the subject in such a manner, that legislators can exercise their powers aright in the preparation of suitable laws, that moralists and theologians can be furnished with facts to enforce the truth on this subject upon the moral sense of the community, especially the upper classes, in order to correct forever such habits, by making fathers and mothers comprehend their responsibility under these circumstances." *

I finish my quotations here, notwithstanding the interest presented by the whole address.

If, besides these American testimonies, another should be needed of European origin, I could cite a statistical work published in 1856 by M. Ambroise Tardieu, a distinguished physician of the Faculty of Paris, a work intended to show the condition of criminality in France upon this special point.† The author, after having shown the facts which he has collected among ourselves, compares them with similar ones which he had seen in New York, and arrives at the

---

* This introductory lecture was also delivered to the class of 1839, and by them printed. The quotations are nearly in the words of the original. Dr. H. R. Storer's Prize Essay on this subject, lately published, may well be mentioned here as worthy of perusal. — *Note by Translator.*

† Annales d'Hygiène Publique et de Medecine Legale, 2 serie, t. v. p. 113, et suiv.

conclusion, "that the crimes of this sort which are committed in the latter city are proportionably much more numerous than in France."

In making the Official Reports in New York his basis, M. Tardieu has omitted to notice two important points, which would have thrown a more vivid light upon his investigation, and brought his calculations nearer the real state of affairs. First of all, it must be said that the police of New York, who determine the facts considered as crimes or misdemeanors, being the most inefficient of all police, many misdeeds remain unknown, or are voluntarily left in the dark. Moreover, the distinctions of the Common Law of England acquitting deeds that in France are considered criminal, there necessarily remains behind the statistics and the Official Reports a large number of cases which, nevertheless, increases this special record of American criminality, and shows still plainer the gravity of the evil.

I think that in France such a crime is not committed, except to conceal a misdeed, which does not therefore imply the complicity of the husband, — a very important fact to be noticed.

Nothing less than the consideration of rendering a service to the Americans induced me to publish these observations, and I shall be only too glad, if, in response to the public appeal of the learned Professor from which I have quoted, I could aid the honorable and persevering efforts of the physicians of the United States, who lament this state of things, and wish for the power to put an end to it. This great forbearance of society in not inflicting punishment must cease. And, besides, the penalties only reach those least patronized, which forms an aristocracy in the crime, and is another privilege for democracy.

XXXVI.

Model Families.

I finish by saying, that in the midst of this lax morality there are still found in the United States a large number of excellent families, where patriarchal traditions are unchanged, and who are happy in all the children that God has sent them. Their life is at the same time simple and dignified. They may serve as types; for they admirably combine self-respect, great purity of morals, observation of religious duties, paternal authority, filial deference, an intimate and touching union of the members of the family, order, well-directed economy, and all the qualities of the true citizen.

It is worthy of observation that these qualities are most marked among *savants*, men of letters, professors, counsellors, and physicians of distinction. Among them the moral qualities are, so to speak, the *cortége obligé* of true talent. One never sees among them, as we have seen in France, men of undoubted talent and recognized worth, establishing almost as a maxim, that a great development of intellectual qualities may comport with eccentricities of conduct, — which are, as it were, the most certain proof of its existence.

This laxity of manners is ingenious in its means of justification, but it has not, fortunately, the power of any great expansion. We congratulate the eminent men of America in not having adopted maxims so easy, and in having sacredly preserved the solid virtues indispensable to men of distinction ; for we must not forget : *talent oblige.*

I was so fortunate as to know intimately some of the remarkable families of whom I have spoken above, and I would render them this public homage as a compensation for the blame of those who are so far from these worthy models. These families remain as the hope of a better future for a society that requires only courageous and devoted leaders, preaching by example, and striving to follow faithfully the founders of this country.

APPENDIX.

I.

On the Marriage of Ministers. — The Ceremony Performed by
Themselves.

I MENTIONED, at page 37, the marriage of a
Protestant minister in England, the ceremony
being performed by himself, and declared valid
by the Court of the Queen's Bench.

An union like this occurred in the United
States, which I will describe; and it is not a
solitary example. A journal published in the
West, the "Chicago Tribune," Jan. 3, 1857, thus
relates the case of which I speak:

"The congregation of the Presbyterian church of Cum-
berland, at Louisville, was singularly astonished a few
days ago. During the evening service, the pastor, Rev.
Mr. Newman, after the sermon preached by himself to his
hearers, descended from the pulpit, and approached a
young lady in the audience, to whom he was engaged.
The assembly waiting, he himself went through the usual
formalities of the ceremony, and was duly and lawfully
married."

Is it not strange to see a pastor putting questions to himself, and making responses to signify his consent? What would the Romans say, such formalists as they were, were they to return among us, and see ceremonies so expeditious, and so little calculated to insure the guaranty of freedom and choice on the part of the woman?

II.

Upon Manners at Watering Places.

I spoke, page 69, of the dissipated life at watering places; but I forgot a circumstance, curious enough to be worth relating here on account of its authenticity.

I remember having met in the cars, at the end of the summer of 1856, a Protestant minister, who, like myself, was returning from Saratoga Springs, — a place greatly frequented by the Americans of all ranks. This divine, perceiving that I was a stranger, addressed me, and we fell into conversation. He spoke of the chapter of manners that we had been witness to, and did not conceal the fact, that the extravagance and life of folly and dissipation that we had observed was not new to him, that it was constantly increasing, and very dangerous to domestic life. I informed him that I had recently read in a paper ("Baltimore Sun," Feb. 2, 1856), "that married men and women now-a-days gave themselves up to flirtation, like young people;" and that, in proof, the journalist appealed to a passage in another American paper, from a different State than Maryland. "These easy morals," according to these two newspapers, "are increasing, and it is time to apply some remedy."

The pastor answered me, "that the fact was unfortunately true, and that fashionable people were only too inclined to copy the manners of Europe."

He added, "that, for himself, the stay at the Springs had for its special object the study of manners, to which he devoted himself each year, varying the place of his observation; and that he always noticed something new, of which he took note." After returning home, he recalled his remembrances, arranged them, and so made material for one or more sermons for his hearers. He thought that in this way he was of greater service to them than if his teachings were always in too general terms. For, attacking hand to hand the facts of the day which he had witnessed, he had more influence in combating

them, and preventing their increase and extension.

III.

Increase of the Number of Female Ministers of Religion.

While this book was in press, there came to
hand an American newspaper of quite recent
date ("The New York Semi-weekly Times,"
Feb. 14, 1860), and I there saw, contrary to
the supposition which I had expressed, page
83, that the number of female ministers and
preachers is already quite large, which gives a
reason for believing that the various congrega-
tions or sects have followed the way opened by
the Presbyterians, and that, like them, they have
not hesitated to confer the sacred office upon
females.   It is one step further away from the
traditions of the Puritans.

IV.

Statistics Concerning the Mormons.

I will say nothing of the doctrines of the
Mormons, that I may not shock the reader.   I

would merely place before him the statistics of
the number of legitimate wives belonging to
the members of the Legislature of the Territory
of Utah.* This Territory, where the Mormons
live, has not yet fulfilled the conditions requisite
to be admitted as a State into the American
Union. It is only a Territory, — that is to
say, a preparatory organization, — but governed
by a Legislature composed of a council (or
senate) and a chamber of representatives, and
by an executive power in the person of a
Governor appointed by the President of the
Union.

The members composing these three powers
were, in 1856, all Mormons, — even the Governor.
They practised polygamy to a great extent, of
which an idea can be formed by the list which
was given by a journal, the "San Francisco
Herald," in a letter dated Sept. 15, 1856, addressed to it from Fillmore City, a part of this
territory.

According to this letter, Brigham Young, the
Governor, had sixty-eight wives living.

The thirteen members of the Council, or Senate, had a hundred and seventy-one ; of these,
fifty-seven were for the President himself. All

* See New York Tribune, Dec. 29, 1857.

are spoken of by name as stooping more or less, purblind, and prematurely old.

The twenty-six members of the Chamber of Representatives had a hundred and fifty-seven wives living, without speaking of those already deceased. Several of these Representatives are stated to be already old. One of them had among his wives three sisters.

Finally, five employés attached to the Chamber, including the chaplain, had twenty-two wives. The chaplain had seven for himself.

To sum it up, the two powers, legislative and executive, represented by forty-five persons, had in all four hundred and twenty wives.

V.

Sect of the Shakers.*

This is the substance of the doctrine of the Shakers :

Towards the end of the eighteenth century, there was formed in England, not far from Manchester, a sect composed of a small number of individuals who believed that they saw by certain

* A Summary View of the Millennial Church, *passim*. Albany, 1843.

signs, that the will of God was again revealed. Soon a woman, by the name of Ann Lee, declared that the divine light had appeared to her, and that she had the mission to diffuse it. The subject of this revelation was celibacy, which according to her was *en germe* in the New Testament, but had been trodden down by men, and ought to be resuscitated and taught, to gain the greatest number of souls. It was under these circumstances, that the "United Believers" (such was the denomination of the sect) went over to America, in the hopes of promulgating their doctrines. There they proclaimed the law anew, developed it, and called forth opposition in order to gain glory by vanquishing it. The ideas of the new believers are briefly these:

Everything in the universe presents the idea of the two sexes. God himself has this double character. He is by himself, it is true, but is perfected by the divine chastity which is the feminine attribute of his being. God created man and woman in his image, dividing the attributes which he united in himself. He ordained them to live according to his law, but Adam and Eve transgressed; hence their fall, which brought all the evils which humanity has suffered in consequence. Generation being the cause of the fall, a regeneration is needed, not only of the flesh, but also of the spirit. Jesus Christ was sent upon the earth to do this ; but, taking the form of a man, his mission remained incomplete. Hence the departure afterwards from his divine precepts. A second revelation was needed — this time in the form of woman — to complete the work of Christ; and Ann Lee was chosen for this great mission. It is not the first time that God has made choice of a woman to carry out his designs. Thus Miriam was employed to aid Moses and Aaron in the deliverance of the Children of Israel, then slaves in Egypt. Later, Deborah the prophetess, had a similar mission in the time of the Judges. Moreover, man and woman being elevated in the spiritual creation from a natural to a spiritual state of being, it is necessary that the head of the church should participate of both sexes, without which this design would be incomplete.

To render herself worthy of this high mission, Ann Lee, who was married, abandoned her husband, whose presence before her would have been an obstacle to the realization of her work and the practice of the doctrine. As a virgin, she would have had no merit in exclusively devoting herself to God, and in making a sacrifice the price of which she was ignorant. Married, it was an immolation of the flesh, which she offered as a holocaust to the Supreme Being. She performed it resolutely, to give to others a salutary example.

Here, now, are the discussions which the doctrine of the Shakers has given rise to.

They say, "Adam and Eve fell into sin because they listened to the suggestions of the serpent, — that is to say, the demon of temptation. Their fault was yielding to sensuality for itself, instead of simply obeying, like the beings of the animal and vegetable kingdoms, an order of things intimately associated with the periodic return of the seasons. God has punished the woman, the indirect cause of the evil, in saying to her, 'In sorrow thou shalt bring forth children, and thy desire shall be to thy husband, and he shall rule over thee.' The selection of the punishment indicates the cause of the evil. It follows that, the union of the man and woman continually offering the same temptations, celibacy is the only means of regeneration."

"But," says some one to the Shakers, "the Patriarchs were married; had children, even by slaves; some had several wives; and yet they pleased God, who, moreover, gave them this command, 'Increase and multiply.'"

"That is true," reply the United Believers:
"the Patriarchs obeyed transitory laws, which
God gave them; but they were the laws of
circumstance, and undoubtedly they carried them
out differently and better than Adam, and, as
the Patriarchs had faith, they were saved. At
this epoch, the doctrines of Christ were not
proclaimed."

"This reasoning," replies some one, "granting that it is admissible for the Patriarchs, cannot apply to the early Christians, who received
the doctrine directly or indirectly from Christ,
and did not live in celibacy. You cannot deny
that St. Paul admitted marriage in express terms
(Epistle to the Corinthians)."

"St. Paul," reply the Shakers, "admits marriage as a last resort, solely to avoid the sin of
incontinence. Thus, he said to the Corinthians,
'But, if they cannot contain, let them marry; for
it is better to marry than to burn' (chap. vii. ver. 9).
The question so put, the choice of the Corinthians could not be uncertain. But St. Paul
previously proclaimed, in the first verse of the
same chapter, 'that it was good for a man not
to marry.' And, in the eighth verse, he repeats
the same counsel to unmarried men and to widows, which proves that the state of celibacy is the
only really pure one, and in conformity with the

will of God. Then, in speaking of marriage,
St. Paul means a marriage more spiritual than
otherwise, as is proved by several passages,
especially chap. xi. ver. 2, where he says to
the woman, 'For I am jealous over you with
godly jealousy; for I have espoused you to one
husband, that I may present you as a chaste
virgin to Christ.' What does this chastity
signify, if we take marriage in its common
acceptation?"

But it is said and insisted upon, "If we admit
the doctrine of celibacy, the human race would
disappear in less than a century, and till then
all family ties would be broken."

The reply of the new believers is this:

"The pretty general opinion is, that the world
will be destroyed by fire. Now, is it not better
to follow the gospel, and purify its deeds by the
quickening fire of its precepts, than to expose it
to perish by the fire of celestial vengeance?

"As respects the family, if in the state of
nature marriage may be useful, perhaps even
necessary to regulate the relations of men, in a
spiritual point of view it must be rejected, first,
because the family engenders selfishness, and
lowers the noble impulses of the heart to the limits
of a small circle, instead of extending them to
all the human race. And then, did not Jesus

Christ say to those who asked him with regard
to the lot of a woman whose husband was dead,
'The children of this world marry, and are given
in marriage ; but they which are accounted
worthy to obtain that world, and the resurrection
from the dead, neither marry, nor are given in
marriage' (St. Luke, chap. xx. ver. 34, 35)."

VI.

With Regard to the Number of Divorces.

I have estimated, page 131, the number of
divorces annually granted in the United States
at about three thousand, and I believe I am
below the truth ; for there are thirty-three
States, without counting several Territories. I
gave, page 111 and following, the statistical
inquiries in several States. Here are various
extracts which, with the others, make my deductions still stronger :

The " New York Herald," one of the most
widely circulated papers in the Union, in its
number for March 25, 1850, speaks " of hun-
dreds of applications for divorce which were
then before the Legislatures of the different

States, and says that Maryland and Pennsylvania (two old States, ranking among the most important of the Union) were privileged in having the majority of these sort of affairs."

The "Courier des Etâts-Unis," a French journal, the most important of all those published in this language in America, said in its number for Dec. 5, 1855, that the Supreme Court of the little State of Rhode Island, one of the oldest in the Union, granted thirty-six applications for divorce in its last session, and these for the inhabitants of only one county of the State, the County of Providence; and it adds, "Judge from this of the number of those who dispense with this legal formality."

The same fact is confirmed by a paper called the "Cincinnati Sun" (Ohio), Dec. 11, 1855.

From a Philadelphia journal, the "Philadelphia Ledger," of March 5, 1856, we see that the Supreme Court of Vermont, one of the oldest and most Puritan States in the Union, granted during a single session, nine applications for divorce, for the small county of Rutland alone.

Finally, the "Boston Journal" for April 20, 1857, reports that the Supreme Court of Massachusetts had granted seven divorces in two days for the County of Middlesex alone.

I might add to these quotations, but it would be superfluous. I desired only to establish the fact, that divorces multiplied as well in the older States as in the new, and that my remarks were as applicable to the Puritan States as to the others.

VII.

Upon the Increase of Population in the United States.

According to the various official and non-official statistics, all founded upon more or less inexact basis, yet giving approximative information, we may consider that the population of the United States increases annually in a ratio much higher than in the countries of Europe, even disregarding immigration. A gentleman quite distinguished both as a historian and an economist, the Hon. Mr. Tucker, has published an interesting work* upon the increase of population in this country, in which he has tabled its progress, in periods of ten years, according to each decennial census, and he makes out the following ratios :

* Progress of the United States in Population and Wealth in Fifty Years, Part I. pp. 101, 103, *et passim;* Part II. p. 26.

From 1790 to 1800 . . . . . 33.9
" 1800 to 1810 . . . . . 33.1
" 1810 to 1820 . . . . . 32.1
" 1820 to 1830 . . . . . 30.9
" 1830 to 1840 . . . . . 29.6
" 1840 to 1850 . . . . . 23.9

This is all independent of the addition by the annual European immigration, which has considerably increased.

We learn from this, that, since the beginning of 1790, the increase of population, great as it is, has in fact fallen off in each of these successive periods.

The causes for this decrease have been sought for, and many given; amongst them, Mr. Tucker has brought forward prudence and pride, which are very powerful, proportional to the great development of cities and the wealthy classes inhabiting them. These causes retard or prevent marriages, and affect in every way the increase of population.

Finis.

Family in America

AN ARNO PRESS / NEW YORK TIMES COLLECTION

Abbott, John S. C. **The Mother at Home:** Or, The Principles of Maternal Duty. 1834.

Abrams, Ray H., editor. **The American Family in World War II.** 1943.

Addams, Jane. **A New Conscience and an Ancient Evil.** 1912.

The Aged and the Depression: Two Reports, 1931–1937. 1972.

Alcott, William A. **The Young Husband.** 1839.

Alcott, William A. **The Young Wife.** 1837.

American Sociological Society. **The Family.** 1909.

Anderson, John E. **The Young Child in the Home.** 1936.

Baldwin, Bird T., Eva Abigail Fillmore and Lora Hadley. **Farm Children.** 1930.

Beebe, Gilbert Wheeler. **Contraception and Fertility in the Southern Appalachians.** 1942.

Birth Control and Morality in Nineteenth Century America: Two Discussions, 1859–1878. 1972.

Brandt, Lilian. **Five Hundred and Seventy-Four Deserters and Their Families.** 1905. Baldwin, William H. **Family Desertion and Non-Support Laws.** 1904.

Breckinridge, Sophonisba P. **The Family and the State:** Select Documents. 1934.

Calverton, V. F. **The Bankruptcy of Marriage.** 1928.

Carlier, Auguste. **Marriage in the United States.** 1867.

Child, [Lydia]. **The Mother's Book.** 1831.

Child Care in Rural America: Collected Pamphlets, 1917–1921. 1972.

Child Rearing Literature of Twentieth Century America, 1914–1963. 1972.

The Colonial American Family: Collected Essays, 1788–1803. 1972.

Commander, Lydia Kingsmill. **The American Idea.** 1907.

Davis, Katharine Bement. **Factors in the Sex Life of Twenty-Two Hundred Women.** 1929.

Dennis, Wayne. **The Hopi Child.** 1940.

Epstein, Abraham. **Facing Old Age.** 1922. New Introduction by Wilbur J. Cohen.

The Family and Social Service in the 1920s: Two Documents, 1921–1928. 1972.

Hagood, Margaret Jarman. **Mothers of the South.** 1939.

Hall, G. Stanley. **Senescence:** The Last Half of Life. 1922.

Hall, G. Stanley. **Youth:** Its Education, Regimen, and Hygiene. 1904.

Hathway, Marion. **The Migratory Worker and Family Life.** 1934.

Homan, Walter Joseph. **Children & Quakerism.** 1939.

Key, Ellen. **The Century of the Child.** 1909.

Kirchwey, Freda. **Our Changing Morality:** A Symposium. 1930.

Kopp, Marie E. **Birth Control in Practice.** 1934.

Lawton, George. **New Goals for Old Age.** 1943.

Lichtenberger, J. P. **Divorce:** A Social Interpretation. 1931.

Lindsey, Ben B. and Wainwright Evans. **The Companionate Marriage.** 1927. New Introduction by Charles Larsen.

Lou, Herbert H. **Juvenile Courts in the United States.** 1927.

Monroe, Day. **Chicago Families.** 1932.

Mowrer, Ernest R. **Family Disorganization.** 1927.

Reed, Ruth. **The Illegitimate Family in New York City.** 1934.

Robinson, Caroline Hadley. **Seventy Birth Control Clinics.** 1930.

Watson, John B. **Psychological Care of Infant and Child.** 1928.

White House Conference on Child Health and Protection. **The Home and the Child.** 1931.

White House Conference on Child Health and Protection. **The Adolescent in the Family.** 1934.

Young, Donald, editor. **The Modern American Family.** 1932.